Active Science 1

Mike Coles
Richard Gott
Tony Thornley

COLLINS
EDUCATIONAL

Contents

What it takes for you to be good at science

There are five areas you need to cover to be good at science.

Communicating and interpreting

Communicating

You should be able to:

- read tables, pie charts, bar charts and line graphs and know what they mean.
- pick out important pieces of information from books, magazines and worksheets.
- find patterns in tables, pie charts, bar charts and line graphs.
- describe clearly an experiment you have done.

Observing

Observing

You should be able to:

- pick out the important things about an object (and ignore other things).
- find similarities in a group of objects.
- find differences among the objects in a group.

Planning investigations

Planning

You should be able to:

- design an investigation to solve a problem.
- decide what equipment to use.
- decide what measurements to take.
- decide how the results would give an answer to the problem.

Investigating and making

Investigating

You should be able to:

- decide what a problem means and how to solve it.
- set up and try out suitable apparatus.
- alter the investigation if it does not give an answer to the problem.
- use the results to work out an answer.
- decide when you need to do more experiments to check your results.

Basic skills

You should be able to:

- make tables of results.
- draw pie charts, bar charts and line graphs.
- know when to use each type of graph or chart.
- read measuring instruments as accurately as necessary.
- follow instructions for doing experiments.

You will get plenty of chances to practise these skills. Each chance for testing a skill is marked in this book with a coloured box.

 means there is a worksheet to go with the topic.

Safety symbols

You will find these signs used in the book. This is what they mean:

DANGER

This sign is warning you that there are hazards here. You must take great care.

EYE PROTECTION
MUST BE WORN

This sign tells you that you must protect your eyes by wearing special glasses.

1 WHAT IS SCIENCE?

Science is about these things:

- observing
- asking questions
- experimenting

- sorting things
- looking for patterns
- inventing

- measuring
- finding out
- deciding.

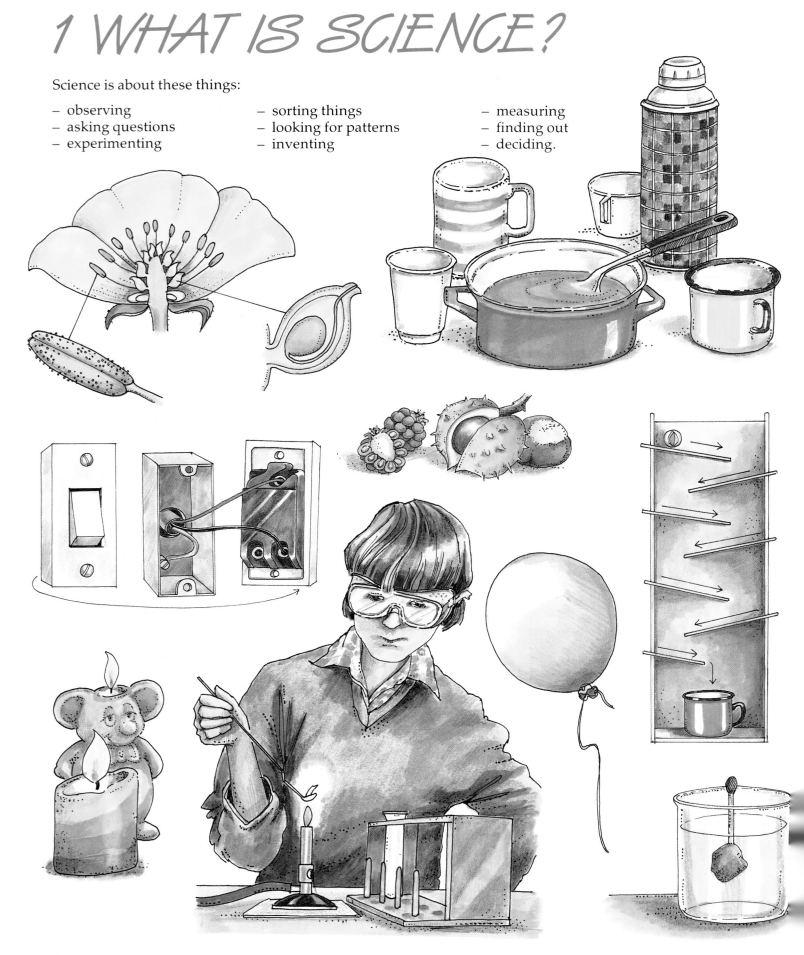

1·1 Fires

- Light the candle and watch it carefully.
- Write down all you can about the wax, wick, flame, smell, colour, light and anything else you notice.
- Put the candle out in as many ways as you can. Can you put it out without touching it or blowing?
- Write down a sentence about the candle that uses the word *melt*.
- Write down a sentence about the candle that uses the word *solidify* (to solidify means to become a solid).

Something's burning!

Look carefully at the fire above. Try to answer some of these questions about it:

1 What is burning?
2 How might the fire have started?
3 Why might it be dangerous?
4 Where do you think the fire is hottest?
5 How could you put it out?

You probably had to guess some of the answers. If you did, then you should check your guess by making an experiment. But it would be dangerous to experiment with a chip-pan fire. You can use a mini-fire instead – a candle. The candle is a *model* of a big fire.

A mini-fire

- Stand a candle in a dish. Put the dish on a heatproof mat. This is your model of the chip-pan fire.

Using the candle model

Here you can see how to put out a chip-pan fire.

6 Did you find this method with your model of the fire? Why does this method work?
7 Think of the other methods you used to put out your model fire. Use them to suggest other ways to put out the real fire.

EXTRAS

1 Close your eyes. What fire-fighting equipment is there in your science laboratory? Can you remember where the equipment is, without looking?

2 Find out what the fire extinguishers have in them, and how they put a fire out.
3 Look at the evacuation procedure for your school. Write down the three most important things that it says.
4 Imagine that your home has caught fire. Write a story describing what you would do. Think carefully!

1·2 Air and fire

Fires need air to burn. You saw this in the last experiment. The chip-pan fire can be put out by someone cutting off its air supply.

But how much air does a fire need? You can use your candle again as a model to help you find out. Your job is to try to think of a way to answer this question:

Will more air let the candle burn longer?

- Put a title in your book: **Planning an experiment**. Now answer these questions:

  - What am I trying to find out?
  - What will I have to alter in my experiment?
  - What will I need to measure?

- Think of a good (and safe!) idea of your own. Ask your teacher if you can try it out. You can use this equipment:

  - a candle, dish and mat
  - some glass containers
  - a measuring cylinder
  - a stopwatch or clock

An idea to try

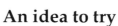

Choose one of your containers. You need to measure its **volume**. Its volume is the amount of something (such as water) that the container holds when it is full.

Volume is often measured in cubic centimetres (cm^3 for short). This is what $1cm^3$ can look like:

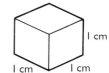

- Use the measuring cylinder to find out how much air is in the container.

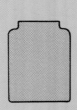

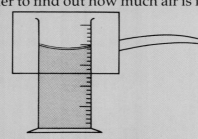

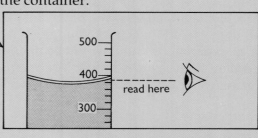

- Fill the container with water.

- Tip the water into the measuring cylinder.

- Measure the volume of water in the cylinder. Take a reading at the *bottom* of the curved water level. How much water is in this cylinder?

1 If the cylinder is too small to hold all the water, you can still measure the total volume of your container. How?

- Light the candle and put the container over it. How long will it burn for?
- Someone in your group must write down all the results. Your first result is the volume of your container, and the time the candle burned for.

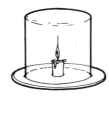

- Now alter the size of the container. Test at least three different ones. Take care to get all your results down.

- Your next job is to arrange and display your results. Here is the sort of layout to use:

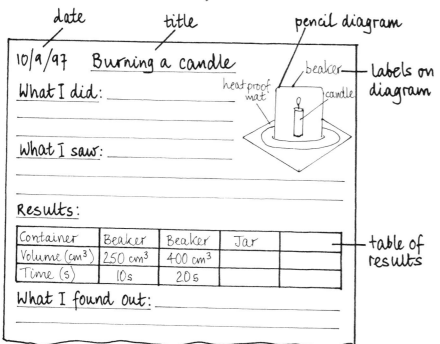

date — title — pencil diagram — labels on diagram

10/9/97 Burning a candle

What I did: _____

What I saw: _____

Results:

Container	Beaker	Beaker	Jar		
Volume (cm³)	250 cm³	400 cm³			
Time (s)	10s	20s			

— table of results

What I found out: _____

Understanding your results

Try to answer these questions at the end of your report:

2 Does a candle need air to burn? How do you know?

3 If the candle has more air, does it burn for a longer or a shorter time? Which result tells you this?

4 What volume of air do you think a candle needs to burn for 1 minute? (Hint: you probably did not test a container that gave a time of 1 minute. Make an estimate from your results if you can. You may be able to test a container of this size to see if you are right – ask your teacher.)

5 Did you get the same results as other pupils in your class?

6 Why do you think everyone's results are slightly different?

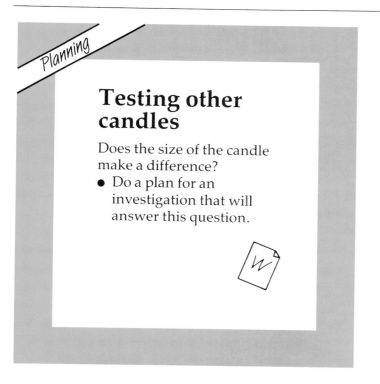

Planning

Testing other candles

Does the size of the candle make a difference?

- Do a plan for an investigation that will answer this question.

- When you have done a plan, carry out an experiment to find the answer.
- Write your report when you have finished. Make sure that you answer the question: 'Does the size of the candle make a difference?'

EXTRAS

You may need to get some help to answer some of these questions. A book or an adult may help.

1 Make a list of ways you can put a fire out.

2 How could you measure the volume (in cm³) of:
(**a**) a milk bottle? (**b**) your bath? (Think of a sensible method!)
(**c**) your science laboratory?

3 Estimate (or measure if you can) the answers to question 2.

4 Imagine you have no electric lights because of a power cut. How many candles would you need to keep your house lit for one evening? Explain how you work out your answer.

SCIENCE IS EXPERIMENTING

1·3 Making a model dragster

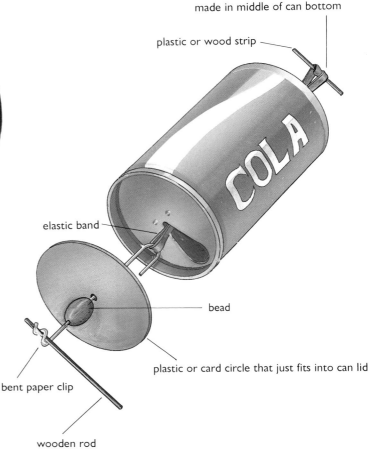

elastic band threaded through hole made in middle of can bottom

plastic or wood strip

elastic band

bead

plastic or card circle that just fits into can lid

bent paper clip

wooden rod

A dragster is a car that accelerates very, very fast. To do that, it has a powerful engine.

Here is a design for a model dragster using a soft-drink can.

- Your first job is to make the model. When you have made it, you have to experiment to see how you can control its speed.
- When you have made the dragster, find out how you can make it go faster. Try not to overwind the power source. How will you find out how fast it can go? Work out a way of measuring its speed.
- Write a report of your work so far. Begin with a date and title, and include a good drawing (with labels) of your design.

Changing speed

Investigating

Now try to answer this question:

Which parts control the dragster's speed?

- Write down all the parts that you think may affect the speed.
- Experiment by changing each of these in turn. After each change, measure the dragster's speed.
- Write down what you changed, and what difference it made each time.

1 Why is it important to change only one thing at a time?

2 What did you have to keep the same to make it a fair test?

- Make a dragster that will go as slowly as possible along the 1 metre course. It must go the full metre!
- Compare your slowest time with the times of other groups.
- Find out why the slowest dragster along the course was so slow. Make a list of the things that made it so slow.

Designing a winner

'Basically, we're looking for maximum grip at take-off', Tony Cook explained as we walked around his latest drag racer. 'The power's got to be there, of course', he added. 'And just a little bit of skill', he joked as his number-one driver, Adam Williams, climbed out of the vehicle and took off his helmet.

'The grip's good, but she's too light at the front again', Adam spluttered as the wind caught his face. 'The front's lifting.'

'We've been experimenting with the weight distribution and the tyres this morning', Tony explained. 'The soft tyres we've got on at the moment cost a fortune; most of the tyre is left on the track!'

'What makes the front lift?' I asked.

Tony looked across at me. 'The improved grip isn't just due to the tyres. We've adjusted the weight balance so that nearly 95% of it is over the rear rollers. We need to move it forward a bit from

what Adam says. He wants better control, and I don't blame him, he's the driver.'

I ran my hand over the long front section. 'It's very smooth,' I commented.

'The drag coefficient is low: about 0.25, I think', replied Tony. 'The drag coefficient measures air resistance. Most family cars are about 0.4. The lower the number, the more streamlined the car is.'

As I left, Tony and Adam were discussing Saturday's British Championship. I wondered how the drag coefficient of my old Transit van compared with Concorde.

Communicating

3 What is a 'drag coefficient'?
4 What is the drag coefficient for most family cars?
5 Why does streamlining a car help to make it go faster?
6 What two things has Tony Cook done to give the dragster maximum grip?
7 Adam wants to adjust the weight balance. Why?
8 Tony says that in the dragster the weight balance is 'over the rear rollers'. Try to explain what that means. A diagram could help!

EXTRAS

We learn a lot about car design by 'pushing' a car to the limit of its performance. It may be a dragster or a Formula 1 racing car. Compare these two cars.

1 What similarities can you see between the Porsche sports car and the Ford racing car?
2 What differences can you see?
3 Write down at least four things that make the Formula 1 car faster than the sports car.

1·4 Sorting animals

It is often useful to be able to sort things into groups. You can predict what something will be like, or how it will behave, if you know the group it belongs to.

Animals can be sorted into groups or classes. Each class contains animals which are like each other in some important way. The three animals on this page all come from a class called *insects*.

Honey bees

Honey bees live in colonies of up to 50 000 in hollow trees or other dark places. Because the colonies produce honey, they are also kept in hives by bee-keepers.

There are three types of bee in a honey bee colony – drones, a queen and workers. The drones, the males, cannot collect nectar or pollen. Their job is to fertilise the queen bee so that more bees are produced. Each colony has a queen. The queen is larger than the other bees, and is really an egg-laying machine. The worker bees gather pollen (for food) and nectar which they make into honey. Honey is a food store for all the bees in the colony.

Bees are well-organised animals and have complicated ways of passing information to each other.

Honey bee, covered in pollen, on a privet flower

Ants

Ants are also well-organised animals. They live in nests, usually underground. The nests seem unplanned, but in fact each ant has a special job in the colony. Colonies have a queen, who lays eggs like the queen bee. Ants eat two main foods: protein, which they get by killing other insects, and sugar from aphids such as greenfly.

Ants trying to move a piece of vegetation to their nest

Mosquitoes

The mosquito is a flying insect. Mosquitoes lay their eggs in water. The mosquito larva hatches in the water and lives there until it becomes an adult mosquito. The larva lives on any food it can find in the water. Adult mosquitoes feed by sucking the blood of larger animals. Blood gives the mosquito the sugar and protein it needs to live. Mosquitoes have special mouths which can pierce the skin.

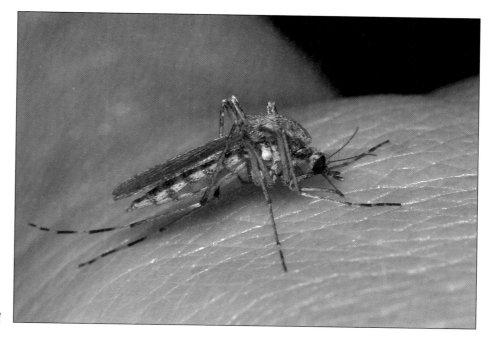

Mosquito biting a human hand

Observing

Mosquitoes, ants and bees

1 Why do you suppose the bee, the ant and the mosquito are put into the insect class? Look for things they all have in common.

Classes of animals can be divided into other groups called *subsets* or *orders*. Scientists put the bee and the ant in the same order, called hymenoptera.

2 Why do you think that bees and ants are in the same order?

3 In what ways are the bee and the ant similar? Write down three ways.

Even though bees and ants are in the same order, they are not the same.

4 How many differences can you see between the bee and the ant? Write them down.

5 Now look at the mosquito. How many differences can you see between it and the ant and bee? Write them down.

6 The mosquito is in an order called diptera. Why is it in a different order from the other two insects?

7 Write a few sentences about where and how the mosquito lives.

8 What special features has it got that help it to live?

EXTRAS

If you have found this section interesting, you can find out much more for yourself from books. Libraries sort books out so that people can find them easily.

1 Find out how the fiction (story) books are sorted out in your school library.

2 Find out how the non-fiction (information) books are sorted in the library.

3 Are they both sorted in the same way? Explain why (or why not).

4 Can you find the code given to books about insects?

1·5 Heating substances

Using Bunsen burners

One way of sorting substances is to look at how they behave when they are heated. In science, we use a Bunsen burner to heat substances. You must learn to use this safely before heating anything. You must *always* wear eye protection.

In this picture you can see a girl heating a substance safely.

- Light your burner with the air hole closed.
  Then get these flames:
  – an easily seen flame
  – a normal heating flame
  – a very hot flame

- Draw and label your Bunsen burner in your book.

- Explain:
  – how to light it.
  – how to get a normal heating flame.
  – how to get a very hot flame.
  – how to get an 'easily seen' flame.

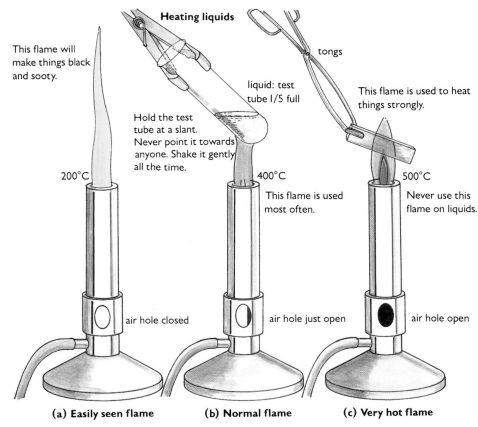

Heating liquids

This flame will make things black and sooty.

Hold the test tube at a slant. Never point it towards anyone. Shake it gently all the time.

tongs

liquid: test tube 1/5 full

This flame is used to heat things strongly.

200°C

400°C

500°C

This flame is used most often.

Never use this flame on liquids.

air hole closed

air hole just open

air hole open

(a) **Easily seen flame**   (b) **Normal flame**   (c) **Very hot flame**

Testing some substances

- Heat small amounts of these substances for a few minutes each in a test tube:
  – salt
  – marble chips
  – zinc oxide
  – copper foil
  – water
  – copper (II) sulphate

What sort of a flame do you think you should use?
- Write a report on what you see. On the next page there is an example to help you.

				Did it change	
20/9/97	Heating substances				
Substance	Before	During	After	when hot?	after?
Salt	White crystals				

Observing

Sorting the substances

- Divide the substances you tested into two groups. It may not be easy, but do your best. Your grouping must be linked to the way the substances behave when they are heated.
- Write down the substances in the first group. Say what is the same about the things in that group.
- Write down the second group. Say how you chose this group.
- If you have time, try heating some bread in a test tube. Add your results to your report. Which group would you put bread in?
- Write down a list of foods which change a lot when they are cooked.

- Write down a second list of foods which don't change much.

1 Why do you think that we cook many foods before eating them?

Working safely

Using Bunsen burners should make you think more about safety. It is very easy to have accidents with hot equipment.

Look at the picture. It shows children doing some sensible and some dangerous things.

- Try to work out what is sensible and what is dangerous. Can you say why?

2 How would you change the dangerous things in the picture?

EXTRAS

1 Write out a list of safety rules for your science laboratory.

2 Design and make a safety poster which tells children about one of the rules.

1·6 A pendulum clock

Timing patterns

Patterns that use timing are very important in our lives. You have an important timer in your body. See if you can feel your heart beating. This is controlled by a timer in your body so that it beats regularly. An adult's heart beats about 70 times a minute. In children it is usually a bit more, maybe 90 or 100. If you are ill, your heart rate often gets faster, so the pattern helps us to know when someone has an illness, such as flu.

In some people the natural heart timer is damaged. They may have an electronic timer, called a pacemaker, fitted. This replaces the body's timer by producing regular signals that make the heart beat.

Other timing patterns tell us how long a day is, and when to go to sleep. We also use clocks and watches to keep time. Modern watch makers use the pattern of vibration of a quartz crystal to make digital watches (see 1.7). Old clock makers used the pattern in a pendulum to make clocks. These clocks were usually very accurate. Some still work well today.

Making a pendulum

In this investigation you are going to try to find a pattern in a pendulum. You will need:
- a lump of Plasticine as a bob for your pendulum
- string to hang the Plasticine from
- a stopwatch or clock
- something to tie the top of your string to

Before you start, think about these questions:
- What can you alter in your pendulum?
- What will you need to measure?
- How will you measure it?

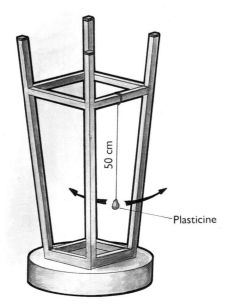

50 cm

Plasticine

Does the mass of the bob make a difference?
You may decide to start by altering the amount of Plasticine. Here is one method of doing it:

- Tie the top of the string to a support.
- Weigh 50g of Plasticine.
- Measure 50cm down the string, and press the Plasticine onto that place.
- Time 10 swings of the pendulum. Count one swing as there and back.
- Before going any further, start a report on your experiment. Look back at 1.2 if you cannot remember the layout. This time you will also need a table for your results. Use one like this:

Mass of Plasticine (grams)	50	100	150	200	250
Time for 10 swings (seconds)					

Fill in your result for 50g of Plasticine.

- Take the lump off, and weigh out 100g of Plasticine. Put it on the string at exactly the same place as before.
- Time it for 10 there-and-back swings. Take great care with the timing.

- You should be able to repeat each experiment and get the same result. If you are not sure of your counting or timing, do it again! Use bigger lumps until you have filled in all of your table.

Presenting your results

To find a pattern in the results, you need to draw a graph. Here is a set of results from an experiment like yours. You can see how they can be made into a graph.

Mass of Plasticine (g)	50	100	150	200	250
Time for 10 swings (s)	4.0	5.0	4.0	3.5	4.0

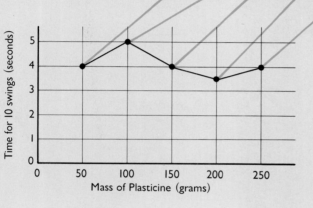

The size of the lump in these results does not seem to make much difference to the time. The pattern seems to be that the lump size is not important.

- Do a graph of your results in your book.
- Write down the pattern from your graph.

Does length make a difference?

- Now do the experiment again. Use the same Plasticine lump all the time, but try it at different places on the string. You could try 25cm, 50cm, 75cm and 100cm lengths.
- Write a report on this experiment. Put your results in a table as before.
- Draw a graph from your table. This time 'length of string' will go across the bottom of the graph instead of 'mass'.
- Look for a pattern in the graph. Write it down if you can see one.

EXTRAS

1 Why was it important in the first experiment to make sure that the lump always went at the same point on the string?

2 What would have happened in the second experiment if you had changed the size of the lump as well as the length of the string?

3 A small clock pendulum usually does 1 swing per second. How could you make a pendulum which will do 1 swing (there and back) every second? What length string will you need? What mass of Plasticine? Use your results to estimate an answer. Then test it out. Try to time one minute. How accurate are you?

1·7 Timers

Unusual clocks

In the last experiment you made a clock from string and Plasticine. Use some of the ideas on this page to make other clocks. If you can think of a better way to make a clock from simple materials, tell your teacher and ask if you can try it. For each clock that you make you should write a report. The report must include:

– a sketch and labels
– the length of time the clock could be used for
– the accuracy of the clock
– the useful features of your clock
– the weaknesses of your clock

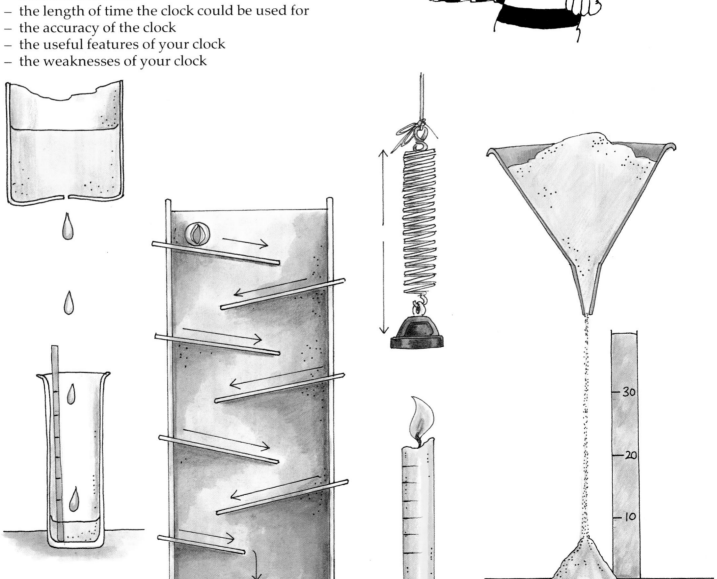

A chip timer

The timing in a digital watch comes from a tiny crystal of quartz. Quartz is the mineral in sand. If a crystal of pure quartz is tapped, it vibrates. You can get the same effect by tapping the prongs of a fork on a table, then standing the other end of the fork on the table.

A fork vibrates at the same pitch every time you tap it, and so does a quartz crystal when it is connected to a battery. The difference is that the fork vibrates about 200 times a second, but the quartz vibrates about 35 000 times a second.

The quartz crystal also produces a tiny packet of electricity each time it vibrates. In a digital watch this is used to drive a chip called a scaler.

The scaler counts the packets of electricity, 35 000 a second, and turns these into one pulse every hundredth of a second. These pulses go to an output chip, which gives you the display you can see.

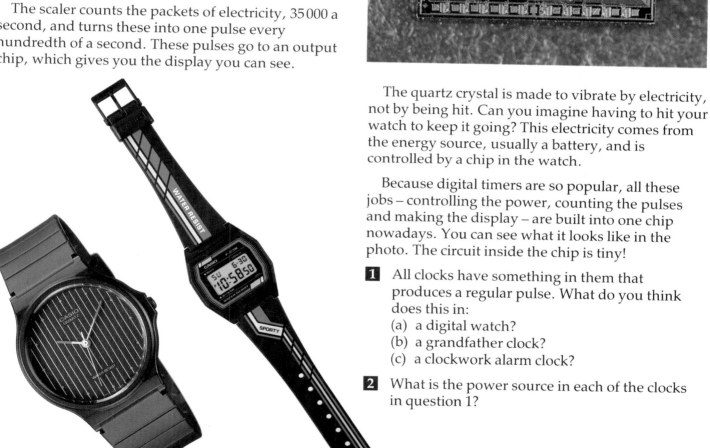

The quartz crystal is made to vibrate by electricity, not by being hit. Can you imagine having to hit your watch to keep it going? This electricity comes from the energy source, usually a battery, and is controlled by a chip in the watch.

Because digital timers are so popular, all these jobs – controlling the power, counting the pulses and making the display – are built into one chip nowadays. You can see what it looks like in the photo. The circuit inside the chip is tiny!

1 All clocks have something in them that produces a regular pulse. What do you think does this in:
(a) a digital watch?
(b) a grandfather clock?
(c) a clockwork alarm clock?

2 What is the power source in each of the clocks in question 1?

EXTRAS

1 Some people do not like digital watches. Make two lists: one of the advantages, and one of the disadvantages of digital watches.

2 Do a design for an improved digital watch. Think about the display, how to control it, how and where to wear the watch, and what it should be able to do. Don't try to be too clever – or the watch will be too expensive!

1·8 How to weigh things

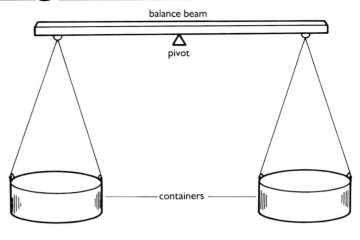

balance beam

pivot

containers

– The scales should be level when nothing is on them.
– There should be a container for masses on one side.
– There should be a container for the thing you are weighing on the other side.

A set of scales

Scales tell us what something weighs. The problem you have to solve is **How can I weigh things?** The design of the scales in the picture should help you to make your own scales. Then you can use your scales to weigh some of the things that you carry around with you.

Your design

First you need to make a design in your notebook. Here are some points to look out for:

– The pivot should be in the centre of the balance beam.

Making and testing your scales

● Use any equipment that is available to make your design.

Ask yourself: Does it balance? If not, can you make it balance?

● Try to divide a lump of Plasticine into two exactly equal halves. Use your balance to see if you are right. Have a competition to see which person in your group is best at halving a lump of Plasticine.

Using your scales

If you have some 10 gram and 100 gram masses, you can use them to weigh things.

● Copy the table into your book so that you can enter your results. Do not forget to put a date and title first!

Object	Mass of the object		
	My estimate (g)	My scales (g)	School balance (g)
Pencil Science book			

● Write down what you think each thing weighs before you put it on your scales.
● Then use your scales to weigh it.
● Finally, see if the school balance gives the same answer.
● Repeat the estimates and weighings for at least ten objects.

- Make a sketch of your design.
- Make a list of all the good features of your design.
- Write down the problems you had in using your design.

- Can you sketch a new design which would be better than your first one? If you have time, try to make it.

A micro-balance

1 Squeeze one end of the straw

2 Screw bolt **halfway** into the other end. If it is too loose squeeze the straw a little.

3 Put the straw on your finger or the top of the ruler so that it balances. Mark this point with a pencil.

4 Push a needle through the straw where the mark is. It is best to put the needle nearer the top of the straw:

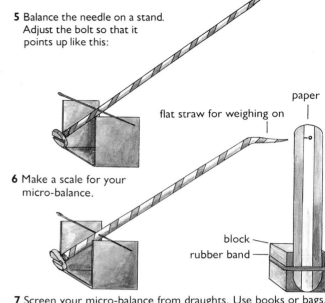

5 Balance the needle on a stand. Adjust the bolt so that it points up like this:

6 Make a scale for your micro-balance.

7 Screen your micro-balance from draughts. Use books or bags.

This chart shows you how to make a miniature balance. The balance will weigh tiny things like a grain of sugar. It needs care and patience to make, though!

Making a scale
- When the balance is still, put a mark on the scale where the straw points. Write 0 next to the mark.

- Cut out two tiny (1mm) squares of graph paper and put them on the flat end of the straw. Mark the new position, and put a 2.
- Keep adding two squares of graph paper and marking the scale until your balance touches the bench.

A micro-balance? Ancient Egyptians believed the god Anubis weighed their souls against a feather to see if evil had made them heavy

Weighing things
- Try to weigh these things on your micro-balance:
  - a grain of sugar
  - hair
  - a grain of rice
  - a grain of salt

- If a thing is too light, weigh ten of them and divide your answer by ten.
- If it is too heavy, halve it until you can weigh it.
- Can you check your answer on the school's balance? Try it.

EXTRAS

1 Old kitchen scales used to work like the first balance that you made. Nowadays there are different types. Have a look at your kitchen scales at home. Try to find out how they work (but don't take them apart without asking!!).

2 Why are kitchen scales *not* designed like your balance?

1·9 Choosing a bike

Science can help you to make decisions. An experiment can tell you which of two things is better. Sometimes you can use other peoples' experiments to find out what you want to know. This sort of finding out, or research, usually involves books or magazines.

Buying a bike

If you wanted to buy a new bike, you would need to make several decisions:
– What sort of bike should I get?
– Will I get a better bike if I spend more money?

– How much can I afford?
– Which shop should I go to?
Where would you get answers to these questions?

Some of the questions are personal. Only *you* can decide the answer to the question 'How much can I afford?'

For the other questions, you may ask friends, parents, look at adverts or buy a magazine. *Which?* magazine does experiments to test and compare things you buy. It could help you to decide which bike would be your 'best buy'.

Study this table from *Which?* magazine, then answer the questions opposite.

| Name | Type | Cost | Frame | | Gears | Handle-bars | Wheels | Brakes | Features* |
			Weight (kg)	Material					
Halford's Pathfinder	Small wheel	£60	—	Steel	3	Flat	Steel rims and hubs	Side pull	c m p s
Raleigh Courier	Roadster	£92	16	High tensile steel	3	Flat	Steel rims	Side pull	m p s
Peugeot Crystal	Roadster	£118	14	High tensile steel	3	Flat	Steel rims Alloy hubs	Side pull	m p
Stadium Topaz	Sports tourer	£75	—	Steel	5	Drop	Steel rims Steel hubs	Side pull	p s d
Hampton Phantom	Sports tourer	£105	14	Steel	5	Drop	Steel rims Steel hubs	Side pull	c d m p
Carlton Corsair	Sports tourer	£158	14	Alloy	10	Drop	Alloy rims Alloy hubs	Centre pull	c d m q t
Dawes Renown	Racer	£211	10.5	Alloy	12	Drop	Alloy rims Alloy hubs	Side pull	q t
Peugeot Roubaix	Racer	£306	10	Alloy	12	Drop	Alloy rims Alloy hubs	Side pull	p q t

*c: carrier, d: dual lever brakes, m: mudguards, p: pump, q: quick-release wheels, s: stand, t: toe-clips.

Take care! The table will only help you to answer *some* of the questions.

1 What is the cheapest three-gear bike you can buy?

2 Which is the most expensive bike with flat handlebars?

3 Write down a list of the special features that you get in a bike that costs over £150.

4 What differences are there between a sports tourer and a roadster?

5 What features make racing bikes very light in weight?

6 Why do racing bikes have drop handlebars? Explain carefully!

7 Suppose you had £120 to spend on a new bike. Think carefully about what you want to use your bike for, then decide which one you would buy. Explain how you made your choice.

Take a brake

Suppose you were carrying out a *Which?* test on brake blocks. There are three types in most shops.

What things would people want to know about the blocks? Here are some of the things that I would like to know:
- cost
- how well they work
- how fast they wear out
- how wet conditions affect them

- Discuss in groups how you can find out about each of these things.
- Write a plan for each one.
- For some you will need to experiment, if your teacher says you can. If you experiment, you must decide:
  - what to alter.

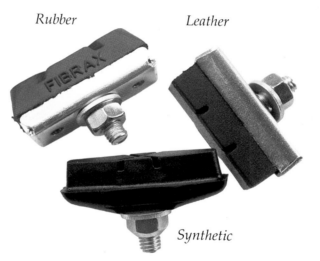

Rubber *Leather*

Synthetic

- how to alter it.
- what to measure.
- how to measure it.
- what must *NOT* be altered.

EXTRAS

When you clean your bike, you probably get grease on your clothes. Washing-up liquid is good for getting it off. Normally, washing-up liquid is used to get grease off plates and pans.

1 Who chooses your washing-up liquid?

2 Why do they choose that particular liquid?

3 What things are important in a good washing-up liquid?

4 Try to get a few drops of two different brands of liquid (or compare shampoo with washing-up liquid). Do some experiments to see which you think is best. Think carefully about how you are going to do the test before starting.

5 Write your results in a *Which?*-style report.

1·10 Keeping things warm

You have to decide on the best way to keep soup warm once it is made. Here are some possible methods:
- polystyrene cup and lid
- thermos flask
- plastic cup
- china mug

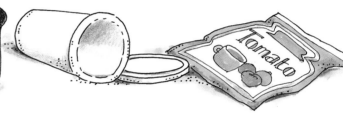

You may not be able to test all these methods, but you can share other groups' results.

You will need:
- Bunsen burner, tripod and heatproof mat
- beaker (250cm^3 or 400cm^3)
- thermometer (0–110°C)
- stirring rod
- clock or stopwatch
- a packet of soup
- a container to test

● Wash and rinse the beaker, the thermometer, the container and the stirring rod. They must be very clean if you want to taste the soup that you make.

Using a thermometer

You must be able to use the thermometer before you start the experiment.

Thermometers break easily, and should not be left loose on your table. Never let them get near the Bunsen flame. This is much hotter than 110°C, and will shatter the thermometer. Never use a normal thermometer for stirring; it is not strong enough. When you put it away, make sure the ends of the case are on properly, or it will fall out!

● Fill the beaker with some cold tap water.
● Hold the thermometer in the water. Read the temperature whilst the thermometer is in the water. It should be about 15 degrees Celsius, or 15°C.

You do not need to shake or cool the thermometer to use it again.

● Fill the beaker with hot water from the hot tap.
● Take its temperature.
● Put the thermometer in a safe place.

Now you are ready to start your experiment.

Making the soup

- Follow the instruction on the soup packet to make the soup.
- The water must be heated in the clean *beaker*, not in the container.
- When the water boils, measure its temperature (**CARE!**).
- Ask your teacher to pour the hot water into the container for you when you are ready.

Measuring the drop in temperature

- As soon as the soup is in the container, start timing. Take the temperature straight away.
- Take it again after 5 minutes, and again after 10 minutes.

- Whilst you are waiting, start writing your report in your book. You will need to say what you are doing (a sketch will help). You will need a table for results:

Container	Temperature (°C)			
	At the start	After 5 mins	After 10 mins	Drop in 10 mins

Leave space to fill in some results from other groups.

- When you have taken the 10-minute temperature, you can drink the soup. Put the thermometer somewhere safe first!

- Work out how much the temperature dropped in 10 minutes. Put this in your table.
- Get some results for other containers tested by your class. Enter them in your table, and work out the temperature drop.
- In your report, write down the best and worst containers for keeping soup warm. [W]

Then have a go at these questions:

1 Think about the container that cooled down fastest. Why did it lose heat so fast?

2 Why did you compare the drop in temperature rather than the actual temperature after 10 minutes?

3 What temperature did your water boil at? Find out if other pupils in your class got the same result.

4 Use your thermometer to take some other temperatures. You could try: the air in the room, the air outside, ice, the skin on the palm of your hand.

EXTRAS

1 You want to take some soup to school on a cold day. Which method would you use to keep soup warm? Explain why.

2 You are running a take-away food shop. What type of containers would you sell soup in? Why? [W]

3 Design a container to keep things hot. Sketch your design. What materials would you use?

2 WATER

2.1 Water from different places

Recycling water

The next time you sip some cool, refreshing water, think about where it was before it reached your tap.

Every living thing needs water.

Perhaps the water you sipped was in the venom of a deadly reptile.

Perhaps it was the first rain to end a drought in Africa.

Perhaps it was from an Indian flood.

It may even have been to the moon!

- How can your drinking water have been in so many different places? Try to write down some ways that water could have got from each of the places mentioned to your tap.

Where is the Earth's water?

The total amount of water on our Earth is about 1400 million million million litres.

Most of it is found in three places:

- oceans and seas (97%)
- underground (1%)
- frozen, as ice (2%)

There is also some water in lakes and rivers, in the atmosphere and in living things.

Testing water

What are the differences between the water from each of these four places? You will have to do some experiments to find out.

- First you need some samples:
  - rainwater (from the clouds in the atmosphere)
  - stream or river water
  - sea water

  Your teacher may have some samples as well. Use screw-top bottles for your own samples. Put a label on each bottle to say where the water has come from.

- You have to find out how the samples are the same, and how they are different. Here are some tests you could use. Make sure that you do exactly the same test on each sample (otherwise it will not be fair). If you can think of other tests, try them as well, after your teacher has given you permission.

1 How clear is the water? Can you think of a way to test this? You could try filling a tube with water until you cannot see to the bottom. Then measure the depth.

2 Is there anything living in the water? You will need a microscope to see very small creatures.

3 Is there anything dissolved in the water? If you leave a drop of it somewhere warm, the water will dry up. Anything dissolved will be left behind.

4 How well does the water help things to float? You will need a float-meter made from a match and Plasticine to test this. Make a scale on the match and test it in tap water before trying it in your samples.

- Write up your results as before:

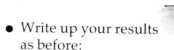

20/11/97	Testing water
Water from:	Pond in school grounds.
How clear:	I could not see the bottom of the when 5 cm of water was in it.
Animal life:	I saw four kinds of creatures.
Dissolved solids:	There was nothing dissolved in the water.
Floating:	The match floated 1 mark below the tap-water mark.

- Underneath your results, say which of the samples you *think* would be safe to drink. **Don't try it!**

EXTRAS

1 Your younger brother does not believe that there is water vapour in the air. How would you show him that there is?

2 If you dissolve salt in water, does the water become cloudier? Do an experiment to find out. Write up what you did and what you found out.

3 Test your library skills to find out about water.

Flood disaster

It is the 31st of January, 1953. At 3 p.m., a gale warning is broadcast on the radio:

Here is a gale warning issued at 1200 hours, Saturday 31st January. All districts will have gale force winds, severe in many places, with squally showers, turning to snow over high ground.

A few hours later, the North Sea broke through the sea defences along the east coast. Over 300 people drowned, and more than 40000 were evacuated to high ground. Thousands of cattle, pigs, sheep and poultry were lost.

It was a tragic day for many people. The Beckertons had been watching a children's programme on their new television when their son Peter came in. He had spent his afternoon pottering on the beach, and had seen the sea start to come over the bank. Peter and his father decided to make sure that the Waltons, who lived with their young son, were safe.

As soon as they set out, they saw that things had got worse. The sea was over the roads, and the weather was awful. Peter got to the Waltons' gate, but the sea was up to his waist. He shouted to his father to go back. Just as he did, a surge of sea water knocked Peter off his feet. He was swept away, and his body was not found for six weeks. Soon after, the Waltons' bungalow was also destroyed, and the family were all drowned. Peter Beckerton's brave but fatal rescue attempt gained him the Albert Medal.

January 1953: flooding on Canvey Island. The boats are searching for victims

Two things caused the flooding of 1953: a high tide combined with a strong northerly wind. The same weather conditions could happen again, but this time we are better prepared. The sea defences are stronger. Also there is a flood barrier across the Thames at Woolwich to stop flooding in London.

1 What would you do if your street was likely to be flooded?

2 Why did a northerly wind cause the flooding?

Protection against rain

Roofs are designed to keep rain out. In most modern houses the roof design is like this:

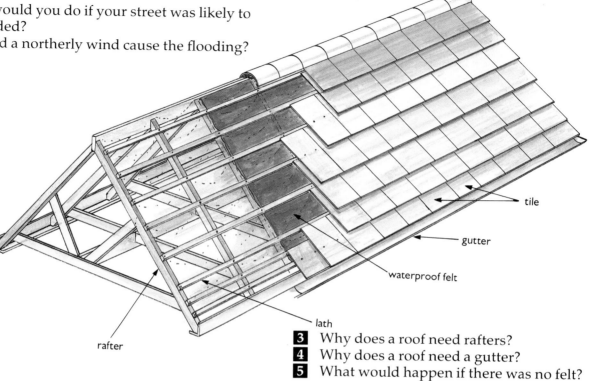

ridge tile

tile

gutter

waterproof felt

lath

rafter

3 Why does a roof need rafters?

4 Why does a roof need a gutter?

5 What would happen if there was no felt?

Investigating

Making a roof

- Do a design for a roof using some of the materials listed.
  - balsa strips and glue
  - 20mm × 20mm polythene squares
  - card
  - scissors
  - a modelling knife on a cutting board
  - drawing pins

- Now make your roof. It has to keep dry a paper towel 100mm × 200mm.
- Think of a fair way of seeing whose roof is best, then carry out your test.
- When your roof has been tested, make a list of its faults.
- If you have time, make a new and better design.

EXTRAS

1 How would our houses be different if there was no rain? Design a roof suitable for a place where there is no rain. Where are roofs like this found?

2 Imagine there is a flood in the street where you live. What would be the first thing you do? What else could you do?

3 Find out how drains take the rain and waste away from your house.

Hot, dry summers

Too little water can be just as much trouble as too much water. The driest parts of Britain are the East and South-East of the country. Annual rainfall is about 500mm in these places in most years. This usually provides enough drinking water. Also, rain during the winter can be stored in reservoirs and used during the summer. But in 1976 the weather in Britain was not usual.

The cracked bed of an empty reservoir in Wales

Rainfall in England and Wales, 1975 and 1976 (mm)

Year	Jan.	Feb.	Mar.	Apr.	May	Jun.	Jul.	Aug.	Sep.	Oct.	Nov.	Dec.
1975	117	31	81	71	47	21	66	52	106	36	73	52
1976	60	40	43	21	64	17	32	27	160	153	83	94
Normal average	86	65	59	58	67	61	73	90	83	83	97	90

1975 was the fifth driest year of the century. Reservoirs were already low in January 1976. In May 1976 the Water Authorities issued warnings that water might be rationed. June and July were the hottest for years. Most reservoirs were less than a quarter full. The sun's heat made the problem worse. It evaporated 25 million litres of water a day from the Mendip reservoir in Somerset.

In August 1976, a 'Save Water' campaign was started. Using water for washing cars, watering golf courses and fountains was prohibited. Water supplies to houses in South Wales were cut off in September. Stand pipes were put up in the streets. People had to go out and collect their water in buckets.

When the rain returned in the autumn, there were still problems. Would the reservoirs fill up in time for next summer? What could be done to avoid water shortages in future?

- Draw a bar chart that shows the rainfall each month in 1976.

- Add to the bar chart, in a different colour, the figures for 1975.
- Finally add the 'normal average' figures to your chart.
- Put a key and a title on your chart.
- Work out the total rainfall in 1976, 1975 and in a normal year.

Water supplies in hot countries

Many countries are short of water all the time. This means they have problems. Fresh water is vital wherever there are human beings. Not only is it needed for drinking, but also for growing food. Water shortage is a major problem for people who live in parts of West Africa, for example.

Niger, West Africa: digging a well by hand. As the sand is removed, the concrete rings sink down to make the well lining.

Burkina Faso, West Africa: woman taking water from a hand-pump

Fresh water from sea water

Some countries with little rainfall have lots of sea water. It is possible, but not easy, to make sea water drinkable.

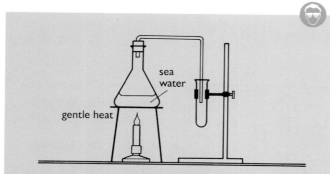

- Collect the equipment in the diagram. Wash it out, then set it up.
- Heat the sea water in the conical flask with a normal heating flame until it boils, then watch very carefully. Take care that the sea water does not boil dry, or boil over. Take the Bunsen away if this looks likely.

- When you have some water in your test tube, turn the Bunsen off. Let the water cool. Is it pure water?

- Do a report on your experiment.
  1 Look at the sea water left in the conical flask. Where has the sea salt gone?
- Do a design for a large-scale version of your experiment that could be used in a hot country. Where would you build your factory?
  2 Not many countries use this method, which is called *desalination*. Why not?

EXTRAS

1 What do you think caused the drought of 1976? (You should be able to think of more than just 'not enough rain'!)

2 Make a list of ten ways that your family could save water. Put them in order, with the best water savers at the top of the list.

3 Design a rain gauge to measure the rainfall in your back garden. Make it and test it out. Write a report on your design.

2.4 Water and life

Plants and animals

There is water in all living things. Animals and plants use it as a way of getting chemicals to all parts of their systems. The chemicals dissolve in the water, so they are easy to carry around.

- Have a look at these animals and plants. Where do you think each of them stores water?

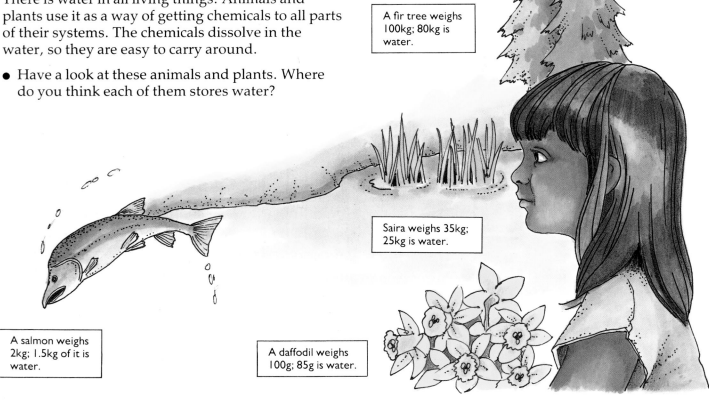

A fir tree weighs 100kg; 80kg is water.

Saira weighs 35kg; 25kg is water.

A salmon weighs 2kg; 1.5kg of it is water.

A daffodil weighs 100g; 85g is water.

Finding out how much water is in a plant

Your job is to make a good estimate of the amount of water in a plant. Here are some ideas to help you:

You can get all the water in a leaf to evaporate by putting it in an oven at 60°C for 45 minutes.

You can weigh a leaf on a top-pan balance.

– How will you measure the amount of water in a leaf?

– Is it sensible to use only one leaf or piece?

– Is it sensible to use the whole plant? What if your 'plant' is a tree?

- Decide on a method.
- Put a date and a sensible title in your book.
- Draw a flowchart that describes your method. A flowchart is a set of pictures that shows each stage in turn.
- Get your teacher's permission and carry out your method.
- Put your results under your flowchart.

Saira did the same experiment as you, using an oak leaf. She found that the oak leaf got 0.05g (that is one-twentieth of a gram) lighter after being in the oven.

Have a go at these questions about her experiment:

1 Why did the leaf get lighter?

2 Where did the 'lost' mass go to?

3 Make an estimate (very difficult!) of the number of leaves on an oak tree.

4 Use your estimate to help you work out the amount of water in an oak tree.

5 Where else in the tree will there be water?

6 Where does all this water come from?

Living things in water

Water is a home for many plants and animals.

- Collect a small jar of water, plants and mud from the bottom of a pond or stream. **Take care not to go near deep water!!**

- Let the water settle, then look for animals. Where are they likely to be? How will you find them? How will you see them?

  A hand lens or low-power microscope will help you. You must be patient in looking. Most animals will try to hide.

- Draw some of the animals that you find. Put a scale bar on to show how big each one is. The photos will help you to identify some of the animals.

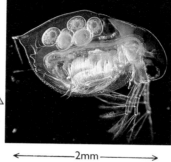
Daphnia ←—2mm—→

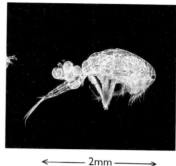
Cyclops ←—2mm—→

Mosquito larva 10mm

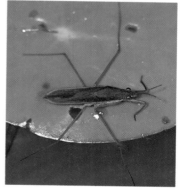
Pond skater ←—10mm—→

EXTRAS

1 Look at the water animals that you found (or look at the photos above if you found nothing!). How are water animals different from land animals of the same size? What is special about the water animals?

2 Think about water plants and land plants. How are they the same? How are they different?

3 Imagine that you are a small water animal. Describe a day in your life. Remember that you have to find food, and to avoid being eaten by something else.

2:5 Drinking water

Can I drink it?

At the start of this unit, you tested some water samples.

- Plan and carry out some experiments to find out which water samples would be safe to drink. You will need to think about:
  - where to get the samples from
  - what tests you are going to do
  Get your teacher's permission before you start.

- One of the samples you test should be tap water. Why?
- Write a report on your experiments.

1 Which water did you decide was the cleanest? Would it be safe to drink? (**Don't try it!**) Which was the dirtiest?

2 Could you see any pattern in your results? For instance, is running water usually cleaner than still water?

3 Imagine that you have no running water in your house. Where is the nearest outside supply of safe drinking water? You may need to look at a map!

Clean water and disease

We take clean water and toilets for granted. But these things have only been common in Britain for the last hundred years. Before that, many deaths were caused by dirty water and untreated sewage.

In 1832 there was a serious cholera epidemic in Britain. Cholera is a frightening disease. A victim can appear fit in the morning but be dead by evening. The disease is caused by bacteria which infect water. It can spread to anyone who drinks the water.

In your experiments on testing water, you could only test for things that were visible. Cholera bacteria cannot be seen with the equipment in your laboratory. They have to be magnified about 1000 times to be visible.

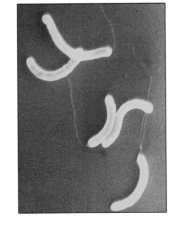

The picture shows a victim being carried away to be buried. At the same time his bed linen is being washed out in a stream.

Between 1750 and 1850 the number of people living in towns in Britain increased very fast. It would have been very expensive and difficult for towns to provide clean water for everyone. Here is a comment about Leeds in the 1830s:

> 'Leeds is ill supplied with that most needful element, water, by its public water works, which were established more than 40 years since and adapted to the size of the town at the time. Only 2200 houses inhabited by 12 000 persons receive water from the water works: and upwards of 60 000 in the town alone have no water supply except from wells and rainwater. The water is raised from the river near Leeds Bridge and forced up by waterwheel to reservoirs. Its quality is very indifferent, and from this cause as well as from the deficient quantity the Commissioners are now engaged in finding some new source. It is anticipated that entirely new waterworks will be constructed at great expense.'

(Directory of Leeds, 1834)

4 How many houses in Leeds had water from the water works?

5 Where did the rest of the houses get their water from?

6 About how many people had to rely on other sources of water?

7 Water was taken from the river using a waterwheel. Draw a sketch of the river, the waterwheel and the reservoir to show how it might have worked.

8 What do you think 'its quality is very indifferent' means?

9 The Commissioners are looking for a new source because of the 'deficient quantity'. What does this mean? What could the Commissioners do to provide a new source?

How water is cleaned

- Convert the diagram above into a flowchart. Your flowchart should use one or two words for each stage in the cleaning process. It has been started for you:

reservoir → ☐

- Imagine you are a drop of water in a reservoir. Describe your journey from the reservoir into a cup of tea. Try to explain why you have to go through each stage in the journey.

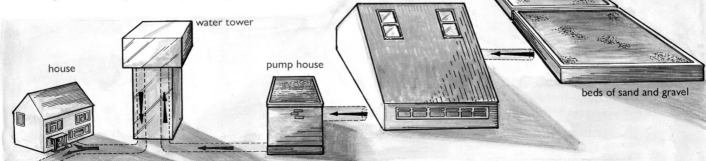

river

reservoir

Chlorine is added to water

beds of sand and gravel

water tower

house

pump house

EXTRAS

1 What tests could you do on the 'indifferent water' in Leeds in 1834 to see if it was safe to drink?

2 Imagine you are in charge of public health in Leeds in 1834. What would you do to stop the spread of cholera?

3 (a) Why is chlorine added to drinking water?
(b) What else may be added to your water before it reaches you?

2·6 Dissolving

Displaying your knowledge

- Make a display with a group of friends that shows everything you know about dissolving. Try to answer these questions in your display:

  - What will dissolve?
  - What dissolves things?
  - How can you make things dissolve faster?
  - How can you get a dissolved substance back?
  - How do things dissolve?
  - Is dissolving the same as melting?

Using water to dissolve things

- You have to find out which substances will dissolve in water.

First you must decide how to test them. Remember, it must be a fair test! All the substances should be treated in the same way!

How will you know if something has dissolved? (Hint: Use very small amounts of the substances.)

Substances to try:

sugar	soap
salt	powder paint
sand	washing soda
liquid detergent	flour
custard powder	copper (II) sulphate
tea	chalk
iron filings	rice
vinegar	oil
coffee	baking powder

Communicating

- Write a report on your work.

- Divide the substances you tested into dissolvers and non-dissolvers. If necessary, make a new group for substances you are not sure about.

1 How did you decide that a substance should go in the dissolvers group?

- Divide the dissolvers group up into two more groups. In the first group, put all the substances that made no difference to the water. Put all the rest in the second group.

- If you have a group of substances you are not sure about, try to think of a better test for dissolving. One idea might be to see if the substance *filters* – a dissolved substance will filter. Try your idea if you can.

Why do things dissolve?

A salt crystal is made up of millions of tiny particles. The particles are held together by forces – rather like the force that holds a balloon onto a wall when it has been rubbed. These forces keep the particles in a regular shape.

Water is also made of tiny particles, but they can move around. When a salt crystal is put into water, the water particles disturb the forces holding the salt crystal together. The particles at the edge of the crystal are broken away. They spread into the water, making a *solution*. This happens because salt is *soluble*.

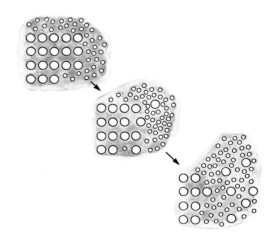

Sand does not dissolve in water. It is *insoluble*. The forces that hold the tiny particles of sand together are different from the forces that hold salt together. When sand is put into water, the water particles have no effect on it, and it does not dissolve.

Dissolving the countryside

The rocks in the photograph are made of limestone. Limestone is almost insoluble, but water has flowed over the rock for thousands and thousands of years. Gradually, it has dissolved the limestone away.

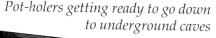

Pot-holers getting ready to go down to underground caves

Cheddar Gorge in Avon

Rivers and streams sometimes flow underground in limestone country. They also dissolve the rock away. Holes called pot-holes are made where the water goes underground. The pot-holes often lead down to caves.

Stalactites (top) and stalagmites (bottom) in Cox's Cave, Cheddar

EXTRAS

1 Look back at the display you did at the beginning of this work. You should be able to answer some of the questions a bit better now. Make a new display in your book. Try to answer the same questions if possible.

2 Stalactites grow even though they are not alive. Can you explain this?

3 What are stalactites made from?

4 Why do you think stalactites are usually longer and thinner than stalagmites?

2:7 *Water and washing*

A perfect wash

Washing then and now

 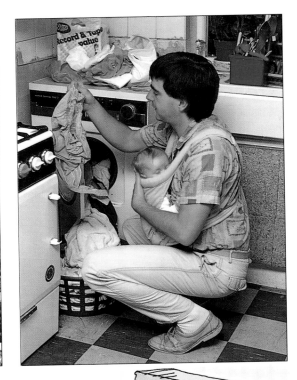

What is the best way to wash a dirty cloth?

- You will need a dirty cloth cut up into eight equal pieces.
- Put one piece on one side. This is to compare the washed pieces with later on. It is called the *control* cloth.

- Now you have to test the other pieces. Some things you could try:
  – Is hot water better than cold water?

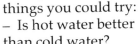

  – Is soapy water better than plain water?

– Is detergent better than soap?

– Is rubbing better than stirring?

– Does 10 minutes' washing get the cloth twice as clean as 5 minutes'?

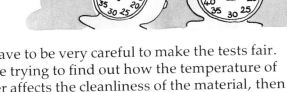

You have to be very careful to make the tests fair. If you are trying to find out how the temperature of the water affects the cleanliness of the material, then everything else in your experiment must be the same (except of course the temperature of the water!).

- When you have finished your tests, write a report. Say what you did, and what you found out. Explain how you made sure the tests were fair.
- If you have time, you could have a competition to see who has found the best washing method.

38

Washing machines

The standard programme on my washing machine runs like this:

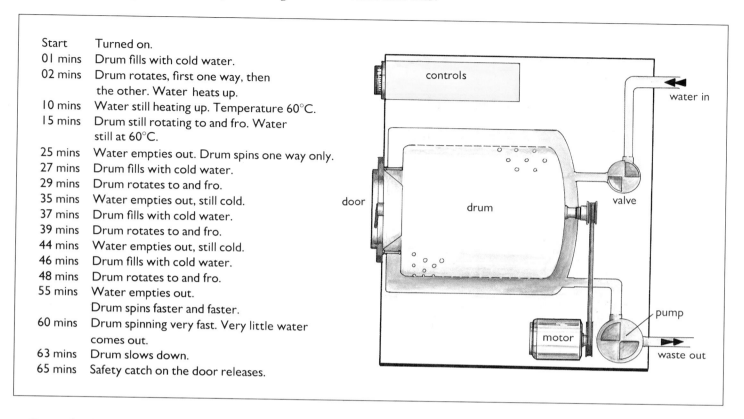

Start	Turned on.
01 mins	Drum fills with cold water.
02 mins	Drum rotates, first one way, then the other. Water heats up.
10 mins	Water still heating up. Temperature 60°C.
15 mins	Drum still rotating to and fro. Water still at 60°C.
25 mins	Water empties out. Drum spins one way only.
27 mins	Drum fills with cold water.
29 mins	Drum rotates to and fro.
35 mins	Water empties out, still cold.
37 mins	Drum fills with cold water.
39 mins	Drum rotates to and fro.
44 mins	Water empties out, still cold.
46 mins	Drum fills with cold water.
48 mins	Drum rotates to and fro.
55 mins	Water empties out. Drum spins faster and faster.
60 mins	Drum spinning very fast. Very little water comes out.
63 mins	Drum slows down.
65 mins	Safety catch on the door releases.

- Copy this bar into your book.

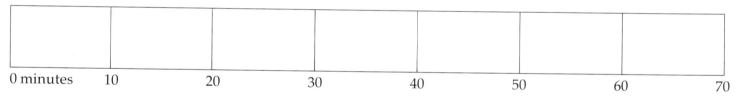

0 minutes   10   20   30   40   50   60   70

- Shade in the times when the drum is rotating to and fro.
- In another colour, shade in the times when the drain valve is open. This means that water is draining out of the machine.
- In a third colour, shade in the times when the inlet valve is open. This is when water is coming in to the machine.
- Put a key beside your bar.

1 A lot of electricity is needed between 2 mins and 15 mins. Why?

2 When is the soap added to the wash?

3 What is happening between 27 mins and 55 mins?

4 Why is the drum able to spin faster and faster after 55 mins?

5 Why doesn't the safety catch release straight away at 63 mins?

EXTRAS

1 You will need a small, dry piece of wool cloth for this experiment.
(**a**) Put a single drop of water on the cloth very carefully.
(**b**) Look at the drop from the side.
(**c**) Put a little soap on the end of a pencil or match. Touch it on the drop.
(**d**) Rub some soap on a dry piece of the wool.
(**e**) Put a drop of water on the soapy bit and watch.
How do you think soap helps us to wash?

2 You have to advise your parents which washing-up liquid to buy.
(**a**) What makes a good washing-up liquid?
(**b**) How would you compare different brands?
(**c**) What would you need to measure?

2·8 Drying

What is the best way to dry a cloth?

Should the cloth be:
- crumpled up?
- folded up?
- spread out?
- somewhere hot?
- somewhere cold?
- in a draught?

You probably know some of the answers (or think you do!). But can you design an experiment that proves what you think?

Planning

Think back to the last experiment. You had to keep everything the same except for the one thing that you wanted to change. You have to do the same this time. So each piece of cloth must be the same: same size, same amount of water, same material, same drying time.

You have to decide what to change in your experiment, and then what to measure or judge to decide on your answer. The question you are trying to answer is: **What is the best way to dry a cloth?** For this investigation:
- What will you change in your experiment?
- How will you judge what has happened?

- You will be given a piece of cloth or a paper towel that you can cut up. Think up an experiment to find out the best way to dry the cloth.
- Write the experiment down in your book. You will be able to use a balance to weigh the cloth.
- When you have written your design down, get your teacher's permission and try the experiment.
- In your results put down:
  - What you did.
  - How you made sure that each cloth had the same treatment.
  - How much water each cloth lost.
  - What the best way to dry a cloth is (from your results).
  - Anything that went wrong in your experiment.
  - How you had to alter your first design.

Why do things get dry?

Drying means getting rid of water particles. With wet clothes, the first thing you do is to squeeze them, or spin them in a machine. This gets rid of drops of water.

But you are still left with a lot of water. To remove this you must change the liquid drops into a *vapour*. Vapour means gas.

Liquid drops turn into vapour particles when they are warmed. Even the warmth of a room or your body is enough. The heat makes the very tiny water particles leave the clothes and become water vapour. This is called *evaporation*. A wind or a breeze also helps water to evaporate. But drying washing in wet weather is not so easy.

Some people use a machine called a tumble drier. Read on to see how it works.

A tumble drier

1. What things in the drier help the water to evaporate?
2. What would happen if the outlet pipe did not go outside the house?
3. Why is a timer fitted?
4. Why has the drum got holes in it?
5. A sunny day with a wind is good for drying clothes. In what way is this like a tumble drier?

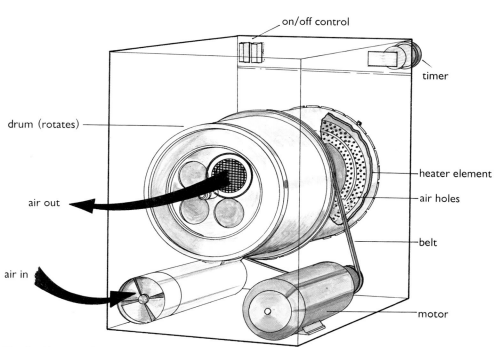

The fan blows air through the heater into the drier.

EXTRAS

1. If you leave the top off a bottle of correction fluid such as Tipp-Ex, it all dries up. Why?

2. Condensation is the opposite of evaporation. Look up condensation in a dictionary. Then write down in your own words what condensation means.

3. Do a survey of your house to find the best places to dry wet things. Make a list of places that could be used. Next to each place, write down its advantages and disadvantages.

2·9 Ice, water and steam

Water plays a very important part in our lives, but so do ice and steam.

Ice is solid water. It is used to cool things down, and for sport.

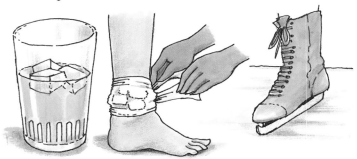

Steam is the gas produced when water boils. We use it to make electricity and in some engines.

Boiling water and melting ice

This flowchart shows an experiment you can do to see what happens when ice is warmed up.
● Follow it carefully. Do remember to treat your thermometer with care.

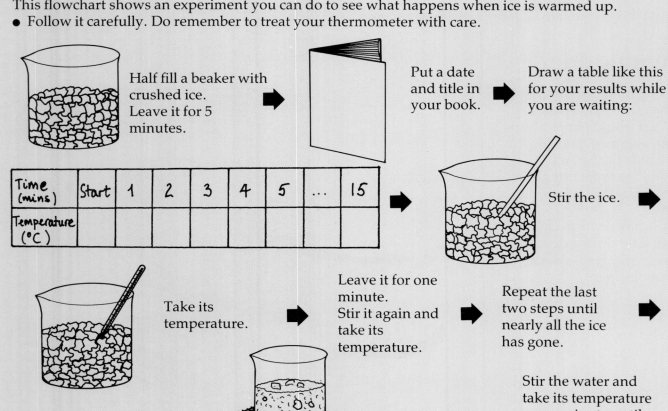

Half fill a beaker with crushed ice. Leave it for 5 minutes.

➡ Put a date and title in your book.

➡ Draw a table like this for your results while you are waiting:

Time (mins)	Start	1	2	3	4	5	...	15
Temperature (°C)								

➡ Stir the ice. ➡

Take its temperature.

➡ Leave it for one minute. Stir it again and take its temperature.

➡ Repeat the last two steps until nearly all the ice has gone.

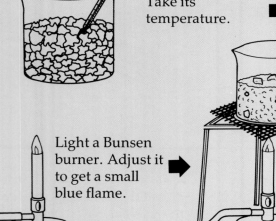

Light a Bunsen burner. Adjust it to get a small blue flame.

➡ Put the beaker on a tripod and gauze with the Bunsen under it.

➡ Stir the water and take its temperature every minute until the water boils. Keep the water boiling, and take its temperature every minute for 3 minutes more. Turn the Bunsen off.

- Write a short report about your experiment.
- Draw a line graph of your results. Put time along the bottom and temperature up the side.

1 What happened to the temperature whilst the ice melted?

2 Where did the heat come from to melt the ice?

3 What happened to the temperature *after* the ice melted, but *before* the water boiled?

4 Reference books say that ice melts at 0°C and that water boils at 100°C. Do your results agree with this? It not, put down the reference figures. Why do you think yours could be different?

Ice can be a nuisance

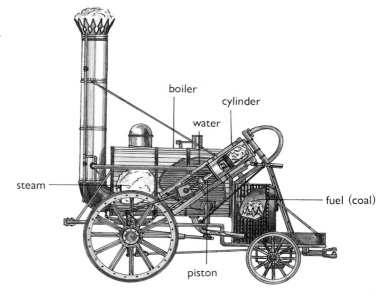

The pictures show some of the problems that ice can cause. There is an important difference between ice and water. When water freezes, it expands. So a block of ice takes up more space than the same mass of water.

- For each picture, say:
  - what has happened,
  - why it has happened,
  - what you could do to stop it happening again.

Steam can be helpful

When water boils, its volume increases many times. Two drops of water turn into enough steam to fill a milk bottle.

Steam can provide power when it is under pressure. The picture opposite shows an example from the early days of railways.

- Write a short account of how the engine works. Your account should include:
  - what the fuel is
  - where the water is stored
  - where water is turned to steam
  - how steam produces movement

boiler
cylinder
water
steam
fuel (coal)
piston

EXTRAS

1 Find out who made the first steam engines. What were the engines used for? Why were they dangerous?

2 What has replaced steam locomotives? Why do you think this is?

3 Design experiments to measure:
(a) the volume of steam produced by 1cm³ of water.
(b) the volume of ice produced by 10cm³ of water.

Do not try these experiments yourself. Your teacher may be able to help you, though.

2:10 Floating and sinking

Do all heavy things sink?

Test as many different materials as you can to see if they float or sink. You could try things like matchsticks or rubbers, for instance.

- Before you start, organise your book:

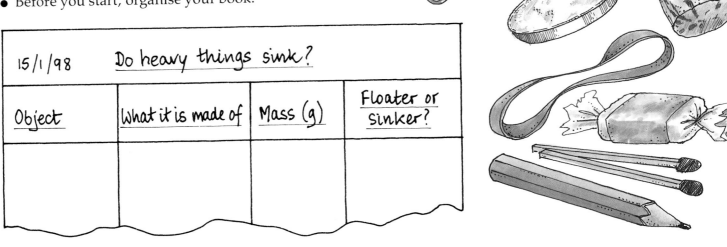

15/1/98	Do heavy things sink?		
Object	What it is made of	Mass (g)	Floater or Sinker?

- Fill in the table for each object that you test. When you have tested at least ten different objects, try these tasks:
- Make a list of materials that float.
- Make a list of materials that sink.
- Make a list of the light objects that sink.

- Make a list of the heavy objects that float.

1 What do you think decides if something is going to be a sinker or a floater? Discuss this question with other people in your group before writing down an answer.

Does shape matter?

Did you put shape down as part of your answer to question 1? In this experiment you can see if shape can decide if something floats or sinks.

- Use a 25 gram piece of Plasticine. First, make it into a shape that sinks. This is not too difficult! Do not let the Plasticine soak in the water, as it will become water-logged.
- The next one is more of a challenge. Make the Plasticine into a shape that will float.
- Draw your two shapes.

- What happens to your floating shape if you make a hole in the bottom?
- Now do the same experiment, but use a square of aluminium foil instead of a piece of Plasticine. You may find it best to do the 'floater' first.
- Again, draw your two shapes.

2 What sort of shapes float best?
3 Why do you think these shapes float?
4 Can shape decide if something will float or sink?

Does size matter?

Do objects that are bigger sink more easily than small ones?

To test this you need:
- the same material,
- in the same sort of shape,
- but of different sizes.

You should be able to compare wood, aluminium and Plasticine. Plasticine is the best to start with, because you can make lots of different-sized shapes from it.

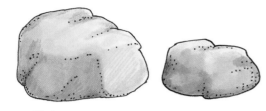

- Break a piece of Plasticine into three: a large lump, a medium lump and a small lump.
- Make each of the pieces into a floater shape. You should finish with a large floater, a medium floater and a small floater. Make sure they are exactly the same shape.
- Very carefully test each one to see if it floats.

- Now test some different size pieces of wood. Do different-sized pieces behave differently?
- Finally, test some different-size blocks of aluminium. Do they float or sink? Do they behave in the same way?

5 Does the size of an object decide if the object will float or sink?

6 Look back at question 1. What do you think now decides if something floats or sinks?

EXTRAS

1 Have a competition to see who can make the best Plasticine float. You will need 50g of dry Plasticine. You have to make a float from the Plasticine to hold as many marbles as possible without sinking. (Hint: Keep your Plasticine as dry as you can!)

2 Do you float or sink? Next time you go swimming, find out. Try it with your lungs full of air, and with 'empty' lungs.

3 Sea water is denser than fresh water. This means that 1 litre of sea water weighs more than 1 litre of fresh water. Here is the density of three types of water:

Where it comes from	Mass of 1 litre of water (g)
Mountain stream	1000
Atlantic Ocean	1035
Dead Sea	1250

The more dense the water is, the better it will support things. What do you think would happen if you did experiment 2 in the Atlantic Ocean? What would happen if you tried it in the Dead Sea? The photograph may give you a clue!

Floating in the salty water of the Dead Sea, Israel

2·11 Water at work

- On this page you can see some of the jobs we use water for. Put a date and title in your book and make a table like the one below.

Where the water is	Why it is useful
In a canal.	It carries things.

- Think of other things that we use water for. Add them to the table.

Making electricity

Moving water can generate electricity. Electricity produced in this way is called hydro-electric power.

When electricity is needed, water flows from the top reservoir and turns the turbines.

Dinorwig power station is unusual because it can be made to go backwards! Electricity can be used to turn the turbines and pump water back up the hill. This sounds silly, but there is a reason for it.

Electricity produced in the power stations is fed into the national grid for distribution around the country.

Even in the winter, there are times when we do not need all the electricity that the big power stations are producing. They cannot just be turned on and off like electric lights; they have to be kept running to meet the peak demand for electricity. So there is sometimes 'spare' electricity. The spare electricity can be sent through the grid to pump water up to the top reservoir at Dinorwig. Then at peak times, like early evening, the water can be used to produce electricity to feed back into the grid.

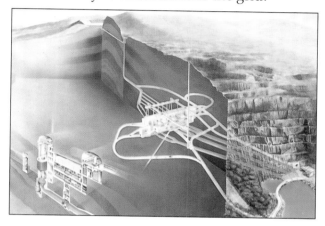

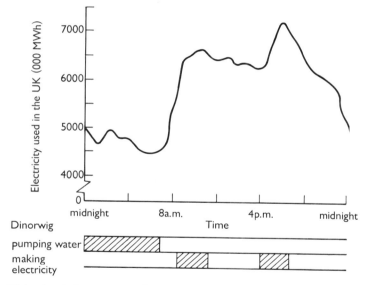

This chart shows you when Dinorwig made electricity and when it pumped water on a winter day in 1985

1 Look at the chart of electricity used on a winter's day. When is most electricity used? Why do you think this is?

2 When is water pumped up to the top reservoir? Why do you think this is?

3 When is water used to generate electricity at Dinorwig?

4 Have a guess at the electricity use graph for a summer day. Sketch it in your book.

5 Why do you think this power station was built in North Wales?

6 What problems were there for the engineers who built it?

7 Do you think the people living near Dinorwig were pleased? Explain your answer. Would everyone have felt the same?

EXTRAS

1 Make a list of jobs that you use water for at home, e.g. drinking, dissolving, washing, watering. Put the jobs into groups so that the same type of job go together.

2 Can you make a simple water turbine? You can use a cork with cut-up pieces of

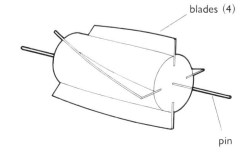

washing-up bottle stuck into it as blades, and a knitting needle or pins as an axle. Try it under a gentle flow of water from a tap. Find out if altering the axle or the angle of the blades makes it go faster. Draw your best water turbine.

Dried food

Most food that you eat contains water. But a lot of the food you buy in the shops has had the water taken out of it. You have to put it back in before you can eat it. Food with the water removed from it is called *dehydrated* food.

Prices and storage times of some foods

| Food | Fresh food | | Dehydrated food | |
	Price	Keeps for	Price	Keeps for
Potato	5p/portion	up to 3 months	10p/portion	over 12 months
Apple	7p	up to 6 months	15p/portion	over 12 months
Peas	8p/portion	3 days	10p/portion	over 12 months
Meat	50p/portion	3 days	70p/portion	over 12 months
Milk	40p/litre	2 days	40p/litre	over 12 months

Communicating

1. How much does a portion of fresh meat cost?
2. What type of food will only keep for two days?
3. Which foods keep for longer than three months? Make a list.
4. Which keeps longer, dried food or fresh food? Why do you think this is?
5. Which is more expensive on the whole, dried food or fresh food? Why do you think this is?
6. Make a list of food in your kitchen that is dehydrated. Put a star beside any that can be eaten without water or milk having to be added.

Rehydrating spaghetti

Can you find a scientific way of working out how much water there is in spaghetti? Here is one possible method.

- Weigh out accurately 25g of the dehydrated food.
- Wash a large beaker thoroughly, then fill it with water.
- Bring the water to the boil, and add the dried food.
- Simmer for about 10 minutes ('simmer' means keep it almost boiling).

- When the food seems cooked, ask your teacher to drain the water off.
- Then weigh the cooked food.
- Work out how much water your food took in when it cooked.
- If you can, work out what percentage this is of the mass of food you had to start with.

- You could investigate some other foods that absorb water when they are cooked. Rice is a good example.

Planning

How much water is there in fresh food?

- Your job is to design an experiment to find out how much water there is in some fresh foods. You could try bread or chocolate (if you can spare it), or crisps or milk or cheese, and so on.

  You can use this equipment:
  - a balance
  - an oven set at 60°C
  - a beaker
  - a measuring cylinder

Weigh   Dry   Reweigh

Some problems to think about:
– How will you be sure the food is completely dry?
– How will you decide which type of food has most water in? You will need the same mass of each to do this, or need to be good at percentages.

- When you have worked out a design, write a careful plan for an experiment. Write it so that someone else could follow it like a set of instructions. Say how to record the results and how they will show which food has most water in it.
- You may be able to try the experiment when your teacher has checked your finished plan.

EXTRAS

1. Design an experiment to see if 'soggy' crisps have more water in them than fresh crisps. One particular problem you will have to solve is that one crisp weighs almost nothing. If possible, try your experiment.

2. You have to cook a three-course meal without using any water. Write out a suitable menu. You are not allowed to use a microwave oven for cooking!

3. Have a look at all the food in your house, or better still, go round a supermarket. Make a list of all the different ways that are used to store or package food so that it stays fresh.

3 AIR

3·1 Is air real?

Air experiments

Air is strange stuff. We can't see it, but it is all around us. To find out some more about it, try the experiments below.

- Fill a plastic bag with air. Try squeezing it and squashing it (gently!). Squeeze out the air from the bag onto your face. *Don't* put the bag over your head!

- Fill your mouth with air. Press your cheeks with your fingers.

- Breathe in and out through your teeth.

- Fill a small syringe with air. Keep your finger over the nozzle. Can you squash the air?

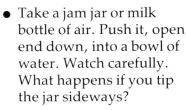

- Take a jam jar or milk bottle of air. Push it, open end down, into a bowl of water. Watch carefully. What happens if you tip the jar sideways?

All these experiments tell you something about air.
- Write down all you have found out about air:
  - what it is like
  - how you know it is there
  - how it is different from water.

Weighing air

If air is real, it should weigh something.
- Use a top-pan balance to find out if you can weigh:
  - a balloon full of air. Weigh an empty balloon, and then the same balloon full of air.
  - a squeezy bottle full of air. Weigh a squeezy bottle with a cork. Then squeeze out all the air and put the cork in. Weigh the squashed bottle.

1 What does the air in the balloon weigh?
2 What does the air in a squeezy bottle weigh?

- Can you do an experiment to find out what 1 litre (1000cm^3) of air weighs? Your squeezy bottle and a measuring cylinder might help you.

Accurate experiments show that a litre of air weighs just over 1 gram. How near was your result?

The effect of weight
Water is heavy; this makes it flow downhill. If air is heavy, it ought to go down as well. What stops air from going downhill?

3 Is there more air nearer the ground than higher up? How could you find out?

Investigating

Measuring the speed of air

Moving air can make all sorts of things move. Windmills, wind socks, flags and crisp packets are some examples.

How could you make a device that will measure the speed of the wind? Your device can be made of any odd scraps: boxes, egg cartons, card, cloth and straws could be useful. You will need something (glue? cotton? pins?) to hold your device together. You will need a way of measuring the strength of each person's blow.

- First discuss the device with the others in your group.
- Then do a drawing of your design and check it with your teacher.
- Then make your design.
- Test it in the wind.
- You could also use it to compare how hard different pupils in your class can blow.

EXTRAS

1 A friend drinks a can of Coke, and then tells you that the can is 'empty'. How would you show her that it is not?

2 Imagine that you are on Mars, which has no air. Read again through all the ideas and photos on these pages. How would Mars be different from Earth? What do you think it would feel like to get back to Earth's air?

3 Do this experiment over a sink! Fill a jam jar with water right up to the top so that it is brimming over. Put a piece of card on top of the jar. Hold the card on and turn the jar upside down. Let go of the card – it should stay in place. What is keeping the card on the jar?

3·2 Living under the atmosphere

The atmosphere is the layer of air that surrounds our Earth. It is about 125km high, but after the first 11km the air is very thin.

We take the air for granted. It is hard to imagine what the world would be like without it.

The structure of the atmosphere

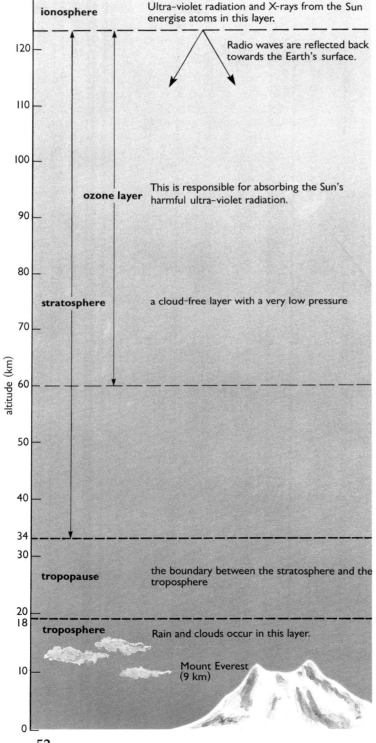

ionosphere — Ultra-violet radiation and X-rays from the Sun energise atoms in this layer.

Radio waves are reflected back towards the Earth's surface.

ozone layer — This is responsible for absorbing the Sun's harmful ultra-violet radiation.

stratosphere — a cloud-free layer with a very low pressure

tropopause — the boundary between the stratosphere and the troposphere

troposphere — Rain and clouds occur in this layer.

Mount Everest (9 km)

altitude (km): 0, 10, 18, 20, 30, 34, 40, 50, 60, 70, 80, 90, 100, 110, 120

Testing air pressure

The air presses on everything it touches. This is called air pressure. How does the air press? One way to find out is to take the air away and see what happens.

Observing

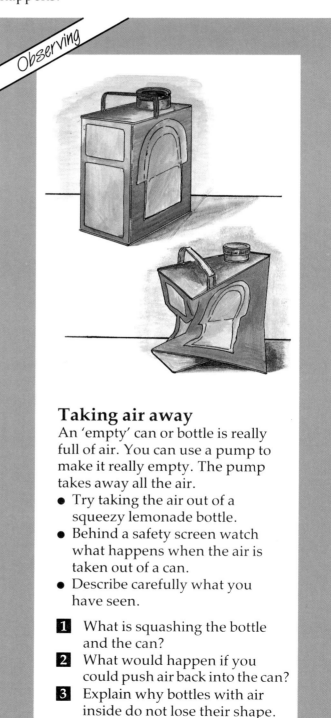

Taking air away

An 'empty' can or bottle is really full of air. You can use a pump to make it really empty. The pump takes away all the air.

- Try taking the air out of a squeezy lemonade bottle.
- Behind a safety screen watch what happens when the air is taken out of a can.
- Describe carefully what you have seen.

1 What is squashing the bottle and the can?

2 What would happen if you could push air back into the can?

3 Explain why bottles with air inside do not lose their shape.

Using air pressure

Air pressure is very useful. You can use it to do jobs that seem impossible.

● Try the experiment in the picture. Take care not to get trapped whilst you are blowing!

Measuring air pressure

Here are some objects that could measure pressure. When you blow into each one, something changes.

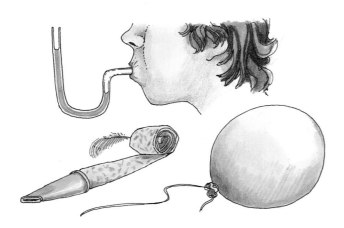

Make a pressure gauge

● You could use one of the things in the picture to measure pressure, but you will need to find a way of adding a pointer and a scale to it.
● When you test it, disinfect the mouthpiece first and blow *gently*. A hard human blow produces a high pressure!
● Use your pressure gauge to find out if a bicycle pump produces more or less pressure than a gentle human blow.

Barometers

Weather forecasters use an aneroid barometer to measure the pressure of air. Look at it carefully.

● Explain what happens in the barometer when the air pressure rises.

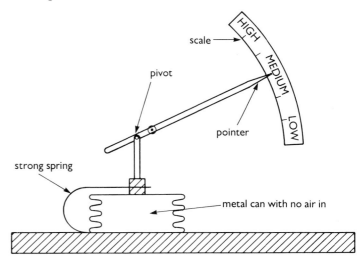

EXTRAS

1 A girl blew up three balloons. She blew five breaths into a green balloon, six into a red one and seven into a yellow one. When she had finished, they all looked the same size. Which one do you think had the highest air pressure inside? Explain why.

2 How could you test the three balloons to find out which one had the highest pressure inside?

3 What is a pressure cooker? Why is it useful? Can you find out how it works?

Uses of air

All the pictures on the opposite pages have something to do with air. Can you say what?

- For each picture on the page write down:
  - what the picture shows
  - what it's got to do with air.

Communicating

Airy questions

How many of these questions can your group answer?

1 How do gulls fly without flapping their wings?

2 What is the link between the girl with a fan and an elephant flapping its ears?

3 What is the link between a parachute and a dandelion seed?

4 How does a vacuum cleaner manage to trap dust but not air?

5 How can the mill operator control the speed of a windmill?

6 How is a hovercraft like a helicopter? How is it different?

7 Can a yacht sail into the wind?

8 Why do racing cars have rear spoilers?

9 How does a bike pump work? What is the link between a pump and a pneumatic drill that is used for breaking up the road surface?

10 A person whose clothes are on fire should be wrapped in a blanket. Why?

11 A motor cycle needs air for two reasons. What are they?

12 Where are the air brakes on an aircraft? How do they work?

- Choose one question that your group can answer well.
- Design and make a poster that includes your question and answer. Your poster needs to be simple and eye-catching.

EXTRAS

1 Have a good look round your house. What items can you find that use air? Put them in a table like this:

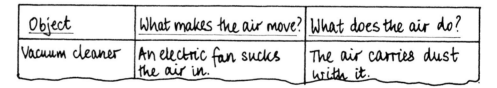

Object	What makes the air move?	What does the air do?
Vacuum cleaner	An electric fan sucks the air in.	The air carries dust with it.

2 One job that air is very good at is cooling. How many things can you think of that use air for cooling?

3 Cooling by air can be a problem. Look at the chart on the right (a *wind-chill chart*). It shows how much colder it feels when the wind blows hard.

(**a**) The temperature is 0°C with no wind. How much colder would it feel if the wind blows at 40km/h?

(**b**) Why does it feel colder if you are exercising?

(**c**) Why is the wind-chill chart important for mountaineers?

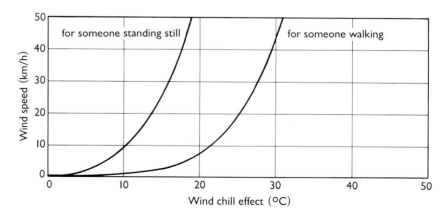

4 Dandelion and sycamore seeds are spread by the wind. Use a piece of paper 290 × 210 mm. Make a shape that will travel as far as possible from where it is dropped. You must not throw it or blow it. Work out a fair test to compare each shape.

3·4 Using air to move

Diving and surfacing

Submarines use air to dive and surface. When they dive they need to be heavier, so they let air out of special tanks called buoyancy tanks. Water takes the place of the air.

1 When the submarine needs to surface, it has to get the water out of the tanks. How do you think this is done?

2 Where do the sailors in the submarine get their air from?

3 A submarine has several buoyancy tanks in different places. Why do you think the tanks are not all in one place?

Something fishy

Fish have a swim bladder inside their bodies that they can fill with air or water. This lets them dive and rise like a submarine.

● Read this story about a giant fish:

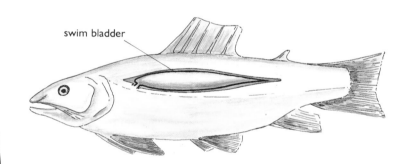

swim bladder

Jaws

The great fish moved silently through the night water, propelled by short thrusts from its crescent tail. The mouth was open just enough to permit a rush of water over its gills. There was little other motion: an occasional correction of the apparently aimless course by the slight raising or lowering of a pectoral fin – as a bird changes direction by dipping one wing and lifting the other. The eyes were sightless in the black, and other senses transmitted nothing to the small, primitive brain. The fish might well have been asleep, save for the movement dictated by countless millions of years of instinctive continuity. Lacking the flotation bladder common to other fish and the fluttering flaps to push oxygen through its gills, it survived only by moving. Once stopped, it would sink to the bottom and die.

(from Peter Benchley, *Jaws*, Pan Books)

4 Why does a shark need a 'rush of water over its gills'?

5 Think of two reasons why sharks must keep moving.

6 How do you think sharks dive and surface?

Moving in air: a propeller

A submarine uses air to move up and down. But it does not use air to move forwards. For this it has screw propellers.

Many other machines have propellers.

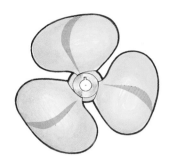

Propellers work by cutting through the air or water and forcing it backwards.

Making a propeller

- Your task is to make a propeller that will push air away from itself as fast as possible. You can drive it with an elastic band.

  You can use any materials that you have handy. The plastic from squeezy washing-up bottles and a cork are particularly useful. The designs of modern propellers in the photos may help you in your task.

Planning

Testing the propeller

- Can your group find a good and fair way to test how well your propeller works? You have to decide what you are going to measure and how you are going to measure it.

- Make a poster to show your group's best ideas.
- Compare and discuss your ideas with the other groups. Which group has the best plan?
- Try out the best idea.

EXTRAS

1. Blow up a balloon and let it go. Why does it move? Can you think of a way of measuring the force produced by the air from the balloon?

2. These turbine blades are from a power station. Steam is forced over them very fast. When the blades turn, they drive a generator that makes electricity.

(a) How are the blades similar to the propeller blade that you made?
(b) Can you see any differences between them?
(c) Why do you think there are so many blades on the steam turbine?
(d) Why is steam and not air used to turn the blades?

3·5 *What is air?*

Finding out about air

Air is all around us. We can feel it and breathe it, and we know what it can do. But even with a microscope we can't see it. So we need to look for evidence before we can make a guess about what air is really like.

You have already seen some evidence in this unit about air. There are more ideas for you to try out on this page. Your group should try as many as possible.

Think to yourself all the time: **What must air be like if it can do this?**

Observing

Experiments

1. Squirt a *very* small amount of air freshener into the air. How does it get to your nose?

2. Press a sealed plastic bag full of air. Squeeze it gently. Put the bag in a freezer for a minute. Press it again. What has changed? Why?

3. Blow up a balloon with a bicycle pump. How does the air get into the balloon? Where does the air come from? What happens when the balloon is taken off the pump? Why?

4. Hold an aluminium foil strip a few centimetres above a candle flame. What happens? Why? Move the foil up away from the candle and then sideways. Can you explain what happens?

5. Look through the top of a candle flame at the wall. Why does it shimmer?

6. Warm up a large lemonade bottle by putting some hot water in it. Pour the water out. Do the lid up tightly and feel the bottle. Put the bottle somewhere cool for a few minutes (a freezer or fridge is ideal). Take the bottle out, and feel it. How has it changed? Put your ear near the top as you unscrew the lid. Is air going in or coming out?

7. Fill two syringes with water, and connect them together. In a sink, *carefully* press the plunger on one. Empty the water out of the syringes. Connect them together again and press the plunger. What differences do you see and feel?

8. Put your hands round a glass flask for a minute. What happens? What happens when you take them off?

9. Take three boiling tubes. Half-fill each tube: put cold boiled water in one, tap water in the second and pond water in the last. Gently warm (do not boil!) each tube in turn. Watch carefully. What differences can you see? Can you explain them?

10. Drop some different types of ball down a tube of liquid. Measure how long each takes to reach the bottom. Why are the times not all the same?

11. Find a can with a push-on lid (*not* a screw-on one). Press the lid down *loosely*. Put the can on a tripod with a safety screen round it. Heat the can with a low Bunsen flame. Stand well back and watch. What happens? Why?

Your ideas – part 1
● Talk about air with your friends.
● Make a poster of your group's ideas on what air is. Don't worry if some of your ideas may be wrong.

An air theory

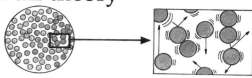

Air is made of tiny particles that are so small that they cannot be seen. Even in a tiny bubble there are millions of particles.

The particles move around all the time. They bump into each other, and into the sides of anything that they are put in.

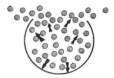

When the particles are not in a container, they spread out in all directions. If they are squeezed back into a small space, they push in all directions inside the space.

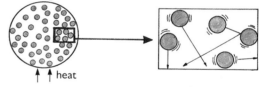

When the particles get hot, they move faster and spread faster. If they are cooled down, they move less and need less space.

Your ideas – part 2
● Look at your group's poster. Are you still happy with your ideas?
● Make a second poster of ideas about air. Try to use some of the ideas in the air theory above. Be ready to explain what you have written to the rest of your class!

EXTRAS

Use your ideas about air to explain some of these things:

1. Smells spread: if someone wearing perfume comes into a room, the smell spreads quickly. Cooking smells also move fast to other parts of the house. How?

2. Balloons are like nets, but the holes in the 'net' are so tiny that the air particles cannot get out.
(**a**) Organise an experiment to find out if any air does get out of a balloon. You need to test for several days.
(**b**) What do you think would happen if you filled a balloon with a gas which has bigger particles than air (like carbon dioxide)?
(**c**) Balloons that you can buy at fairs float in the air. These are filled with a gas called helium that has very small particles. Why are the fair balloons made of tin foil and not rubber?

3.6 The ingredients of air

An important discovery

Until just over two hundred years ago, all gases were called 'airs'. No one knew what air was made of. There were some strange ideas!

People thought air was a single substance. A scientist made a strong-smelling gas called ammonia. He thought it was just an impurity in the air! Hydrogen, a gas which burns easily, was called 'inflammable air'.

Two hundred years ago, only one or two people had the time and money to do scientific experiments. Nearly all of them were men. These days many more people are involved in science, both women and men. You could become one of them when you leave school!

In the 1700s there was a man who did experiments with 'airs'. He was the Reverend Dr Joseph Priestley. He was a well-disciplined man. He did not drink alcohol, only ate vegetables, and was not easy to get on with. His normal clothes included a cocked hat, powdered wig and brass-buckled shoes. If you are safety-minded, you will be pleased to hear that he took these off for his experiments.

One Sunday in August 1774, he focused the Sun's rays to heat up some red powder in a glass flask. (There was no Bunsen burner or gas supply then!) After his sermon that evening, he thought about what he had seen. An 'air', with no colour, had come from the red powder, leaving behind a silvery liquid metal. Priestley wrote: 'What surprised me more than I can well express was that a candle burned in this air with a remarkably brilliant flame.'

Priestley put a mouse in a jar of the gas, and saw that the animal became very full of life. And he tried breathing the gas himself.

Every year Priestley went to France (quite a long and difficult journey without aircraft or big ships). On one trip he met a French lawyer called Antoine Lavoisier. This young man was interested in chemicals and burning. He had already found out

Joseph Priestley

Antoine Lavoisier

that only part of the air is used up when something burns in it.

Priestley told Lavoisier about the special gas he had found. Lavoisier was very excited. He could now explain a lot more about burning. He repeated Priestley's experiments, and made a theory of combustion, or burning. His ideas are still used today. He called Priestley's gas *oxygen*. The other part of the air which does not support life or burning he called *azote*, which means 'without life'. Nowadays we call that gas *nitrogen*.

In 1794 Antoine Lavoisier was put to death in the French Revolution. The judge at his trial said, 'France does not need men of science.'

How much oxygen is in the air?

You can use a candle to burn up oxygen in a container filled with air. What is left should be almost all nitrogen.

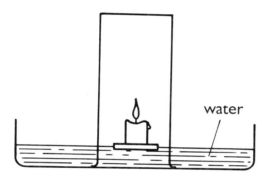
water

- Use the diagram to design an experiment to find out how much oxygen is in the air. Think carefully:
  - what apparatus you will need.
  - what you will have to measure.
  - how you will check your result.
- Carry out the experiment.
- Write up your experiment properly (date, title, what you did, what you saw, what you found out). Look back at 1.2 if you cannot remember how to do this.
- Work out how much oxygen you think there is in 1000cm³ of air.
- Discuss with your group why your result might not be right. Put your ideas in your report.

What else is in the air?

The most common gases in the air are:

nitrogen   78%
oxygen   21%
rare gases (argon, neon, helium, krypton, xenon, radon)   1%
carbon dioxide   0.03%

Did you get the amount of oxygen right? One reason why you may not have done is that the candle does not burn up all the oxygen.

- Make a pie chart that shows the *main gases* in the air.

There are other things in the air in very small quantities. Sulphur dioxide, nitrogen oxides, dust and smoke are examples. Most of the extra things are unwelcome and cause pollution.

EXTRAS

1 There are some other 'inactive' gases in the air apart from nitrogen. What are the names of the inactive gases? Find out what they are used for.

2 Think of an experiment to measure how much oxygen there is in the air that you breathe out.

3 Do you think that the world 'does not need men of science'? What would the world be like without them?

3·7 Oxygen

Substances that burn in air will burn faster in oxygen. Oxy-acetylene torches can cut metal very fast: the hot metal burns in the oxygen-rich gas. You can try burning some substances in oxygen, but you must take care. Think **safe** all the time.

Burning things in oxygen

You must wear eye protection. You must protect your table with heatproof mats.

You can burn some of these substances:
- copper
- iron wool
- sulphur (use only a rice-grain-sized piece, because the gas produced is very poisonous)
- a spill
- magnesium (do not look directly at burning magnesium, or it may blind you)

● Heat each of these substances in turn until it is red hot or catches fire. Then put it quickly into a test-tube of oxygen. The picture here should help you to do this safely.

Oxy-acetylene being used to cut through steel

● Write a report on what you see. For each substance, say what it was like before, during and after heating.

All the substances that you burnt produce *oxides*. Copper, magnesium and iron oxides are powders.

The spill and the sulphur make oxides as well, but they are gases. Sulphur oxide is a very poisonous gas.

When the spill burns, it makes hydrogen oxide and carbon dioxide. Liquid hydrogen oxide is better known as water.

You can test for carbon dioxide gas by shaking it in a tube with some limewater. The limewater will go cloudy if carbon dioxide is mixed with it.

1 How could you show that a burning spill makes carbon dioxide and hydrogen oxide? Design an experiment to do this. Get your teacher to check it, then carry it out and write it up.

2 A friend says that burning has nothing to do with the oxides. She says they are in the spill and come out later. How would you show that she is wrong?

3 In Priestley's experiment in 3.6 he used the heat of the sun to change a red powder into oxygen. He was doing the opposite of burning. What was the silver metal he made? What do you think the red powder was?

Observing

Observing burning

When something burns, lots of things happen.

- Think of a burning match. What would you notice? Make a list of everything you can think of.

- Now plan an experiment to see how things burn. Get your teacher to approve your plan. Before you start, decide on a way of recording all the things that may happen.
- Burn a tiny piece of each substance in turn.

- Write a report of your experiment.
- Make four groups in your book:
  – substances that made flames
  – substances that made ash
  – substances that made smoke
  – substances that were easy to light.
  Try to put each substance you tested into at least one of these groups. Some may have to go under all four headings. Some will not go under any.

EXTRAS: combustion

Combustion means burning. A car burns petrol inside its engine.

1 A car engine is called an internal combustion engine. Explain:
(a) why it is a combustion engine
(b) why the combustion is *internal*.

2 Think of an example, or do a design, of an engine that produces movement from external combustion.

3 There are over 20 million internal combustion engines in Britain at the moment. What problems do they cause?

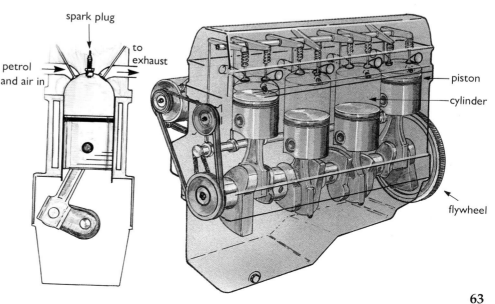

spark plug
to exhaust
petrol and air in
piston
cylinder
flywheel

3·8 Breathing 1

Fire!

'Being a fire officer is frustrating. You can feel so helpless. Take this lad we've just carried out of the building. He's still warm, and I've tried all I know to get him breathing. All I can do now is let the doc do her stuff. And my head is spinning . . .'

'Have you cleared out the lungs?' the doctor asked.

'Yes,' I said in a voice that didn't sound like mine. 'We gave him a good clear-out before we tried the oxygen.'

'Where was he? On the floor? Did he have much air? How thick was the smoke? Any toxic fumes? Did he vomit?'

'No, no, he didn't.' The questions came thick and fast, but not as fast as the doctor's brain was working. 'I gave him mouth-to-mouth for . . .'

'But no signs?' she interrupted.

The doctor pumped the lad's chest while the ambulance man tried a breathing machine. At the same time another ambulance man prepared to move the poor fellow into the ambulance. They were soon racing off to the Infirmary.

'Any signs?' whispered a constable as he turned away from where the lad had been.

'Don't think so,' I heard myself reply. 'I hope he's OK, not just another of the thousands who don't survive the smoke each year.'

Death by choking

In 1984, 766 people died in fires in Britain. Of these, 38 died from asphyxiation, which is another word for suffocation.

The fire uses up the oxygen in the air, leaving none for the victims to breathe. Their lungs fill with smoke.

Imagine that you are a doctor called to a fire.

1 What would you do when you arrived at the fire?
2 What would you ask the fire officer?
3 What tests would you do on any victim brought out of the fire?

Why do we breathe?

We breathe oxygen. The oxygen combines with food stores in our body to produce:
- energy to move our muscles
- carbon dioxide
- water.

This process is called respiration.

Respiration and combustion

In 3.7 you had to show that a candle produced two oxides when it burned.

4 Can you remember what the oxides were and how you showed it?

- Design an experiment to show that we breathe out more carbon dioxide than we breathe in.
- When you have done the design, get your teacher to approve it and then try the experiment out.
- Think of a way to show that we breathe out water vapour. (Hint if you get stuck: you can see water vapour when it is **cold**.)
- Do a sketch in your book to show what happens when a candle burns. Show what is needed for it to burn, and what is made when it burns.
- Then do a second sketch which shows what happens when you respire.
- Make a list of the similarities between a candle burning and you respiring.
- Make another list of the differences.

EXTRAS:
How good are your lungs?

It is not easy to compare the lung power of different people. These experiments will give you a rough idea how good your lungs are.

1 Use a balloon that has been well stretched. See how big you can make it with one breath. Do this sitting down, and dip the open end of the balloon in antiseptic before trying it. Can you find a way of measuring how much air you have breathed into the balloon? Compare your result with other children in your class. You should all use the same balloon. Why? Remember to dip it in antiseptic each time.

2 Measure your breathing rate for one minute sitting down. Then get a friend to hold a chair steady while you step on and off it as fast as you can for one minute. (Take care, and don't over-exert yourself.) ⚠ Measure your breathing again for one minute as soon as you stop. Find out how long it takes for your breathing to return to your resting rate.

Using a meter to measure how fast the lungs can breathe out air

3·9 Breathing 2

How do you breathe?

Air is pulled into your lungs by muscles that surround your chest. Inside the lungs, some of the oxygen moves from the air into your blood, and some of the carbon dioxide in your blood goes into the air. This air is then squeezed out of the lungs.

So when you breathe, two things happen:
- muscles move air in and out of your lungs
- oxygen and carbon dioxide change places in your lungs.

The rib-cage muscles and the diaphragm muscle move the air in.

The volume of the lungs gets bigger. Air is pulled into them.

The air travels down smaller and smaller tubes. At the end of these tubes are tiny bags of air called alveoli. These bags have small blood vessels all over them.

Oxygen moves into the blood. Carbon dioxide moves into the air.

The rib muscles and the diaphragm muscle relax, and air is pushed out of the lungs and out of your mouth and nose.

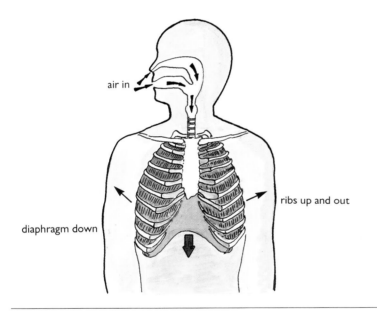

air in

ribs up and out

diaphragm down

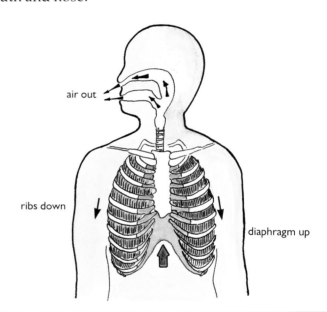

air out

ribs down

diaphragm up

How much do you breathe?

- You will need to do some experiments with your own breathing to answer the question below. Think carefully
- *what* you are trying to do and
- *what* you will need to measure. Get your teacher's approval before you start.

1 How many times do you breathe out in a minute?
2 How much air do you breathe out in a normal breath?
- Use your own results to work out how much air you breathe out in one minute.

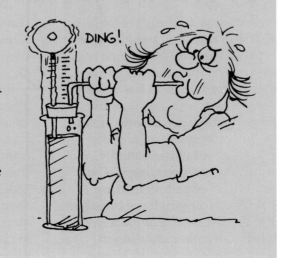

- Find out the results of everyone in your class. Make them into a bar chart that shows the results for all your class. Colour the girls' results in blue and the boys' results in red.
- Use your chart to find out if girls breathe more air in a minute than boys. Can you explain your result?

DING!

Gasping . . . for air . . .

Below: Some newborn babies need help with their breathing
Right: Child using an inhaler to control an asthma attack

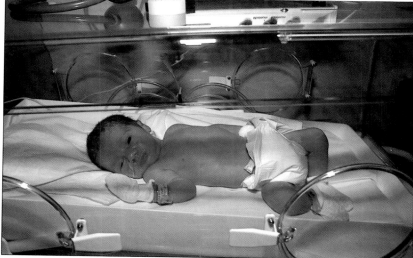

Many people do not find breathing easy. If your chest muscles stop working, a machine has to be used to force air in and out of the lungs. Polio is one disease that can cause paralysis of the chest muscles. It is very rare now, as all children are vaccinated against it.

About one in ten children suffers from asthma. There is probably at least one asthmatic in your class.

Asthmatics have normal chest muscles, but the airways in their lungs can suddenly become very narrow. This may be caused by many things: dust, pollen, animal fur, exercise and some food additives have all been linked with asthma.

In a bad asthma attack, the airways may narrow so much that the asthmatic gets desperate for breath. His or her breathing becomes fast and very shallow. It becomes very tiring and a real effort just to get enough air to stay alive.

Most asthmatics have inhalers to prevent this. The inhalers contain drugs that relax the chest muscles and make breathing easier. There are also drugs that coat the lining of the airways to stop them narrowing.

Many children who have asthma grow out of it as they get older. Why do you think this is?

Asthma treatment has improved a lot in recent years. But we still do not know exactly why it happens. A lot more research is still needed before we can cure the disease.

- Explain how asthma differs from paralysis of the chest muscles.
- **3** Why does asthma make breathing difficult?
- **4** How is chest paralysis treated?
- **5** How is asthma treated?
- Imagine you can hardly get enough air into your lungs to stay alive. Write a few lines to describe what it feels like.

EXTRAS

1 Feel your ribs while you are breathing. What happens to them? Do you have to make more of an effort to breathe in or to breathe out?

Investigating

2 Do an experiment at home to find out if old people breathe faster than young people. Think carefully – it must be a *fair* test. Write up your results. Explain how you made sure it was a fair experiment.

Fire damage

Every year insurance companies pay out millions of pounds to replace property lost in fires. Much of this damage is caused by smoke, and by the methods used to put the fire out.

The fire service is always searching for ways of reducing fire damage. One method that they use is ventilation. They let air into the building that is on fire. This sounds very strange: air is just what the fire needs to *burn*.

Mushrooming

1. Hot air goes up. In a building which is on fire, the hot air rises as far as it can.

2. Hot gases rise up staircases and lift shafts. As they move upwards, they spread the fire because of the heat. This is called *mushrooming*. It is one of the most common causes of fire spread.

3. Fire-fighters open up the building using doors, windows and skylights. This clears the hot air and smoke; it also makes it easier for the fire-fighters to see.

Opening the building up gives the fire more oxygen. It may make it burn faster. It could also put nearby buildings at risk. But in the early stages of a fire, more air makes little difference to the rate of burning. So ventilation is sensible before the fire has a real hold.

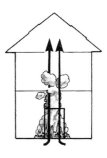

How do fire-fighters ventilate a fire?

Ventilation starts at the top. The chief fire officer must find out what the building is like first. He will want to know about staircases and lift shafts in particular. He may ask for a skylight to be opened. He may even ask for part of the roof to be removed to make a hole at the top. If possible, he will make many small openings instead of one large hole.

Then the lowest doors and windows are opened. The weather and wind help him to decide how many to open. For example, if it is very humid or muggy, smoke will not rise quickly. So in humid weather the fire officer will open more windows.

Some fire-fighters will work inside the building if possible. Their job is to find and tackle the root of the fire. Other fire-fighters use hoses outside. They never direct their hoses through the ventilation openings at the top of the building. If they did, the hot gas and smoke would be pushed back onto the fire-fighters inside the building.

1. Why does it sound 'very strange' that fire-fighters ventilate burning buildings?
2. How does 'opening up a building' help?
3. Why may ventilating a building put other buildings at risk?
4. Write out a list of jobs for a chief fire officer at a fire. Put them in order, with the most urgent job first.
5. 'In the early stages, more air makes little difference to the rate of burning.' Why do you think this is?
6. The fire-fighters make holes at the top first. Then they open doors and windows at the bottom. Why do they do it in that order?
7. You should close doors in your home at night, and when you go away. Why?

Testing chimneys

The job of a chimney is to pull as much air up as possible. Your class can work together to find out the best design for a chimney.

- Before you start, answer these questions:
  - How can you estimate how well a chimney is working?
  - What should you use as a 'fire'?
  - Will a tall chimney work better than a small one?
  - Will a thin chimney work better than a fat one?
  - Should the chimney be straight or at an angle?
  - What happens if the chimney is partly blocked?
- Do a sketch and explain how you would test some of these ideas.
- Your class can then try some of them out with your teacher's help.

Which of your ideas were right?

EXTRA
heat at home

Find out how air moves around your living room at home. It is best to do it when the room is being heated. A very light and small piece of tissue will show you which way the air is moving.

Do an elevation drawing of the room. An elevation is a view from the side: what you would see if a side wall was taken out. On your elevation, draw arrows to show the flow of air.

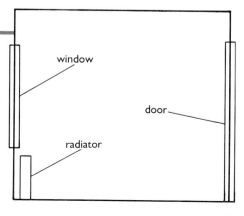

Under water

Some people do not have normal air to breathe. They have to work where there is little or no air: in space or under water.

The longest that a person has survived under water without air is 13 mins 42.5 secs. Pearl divers are very good at this. They stay under for as long as possible, searching for oysters with pearls in.

Other humans need to spend longer under water. If you want to hunt fish, to explore sunken ships or to build and repair offshore oil rigs, you need your own supply of air.

Japanese woman diving for pearls, and an American diver with oxygen equipment

Air supplies

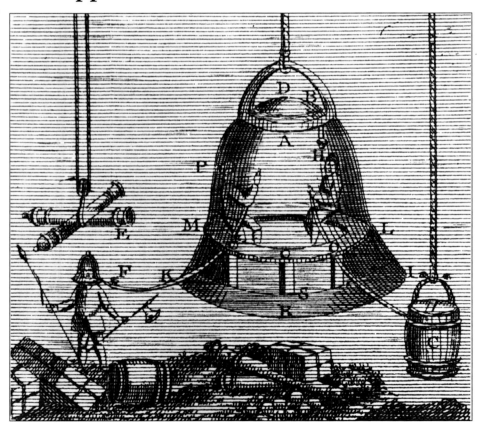

An 18th century design for a diving bell. Two people sit in the bell and air is fed in through a tube from the barrel (right). The person outside has a helmet with a breathing tube connected to the diving bell. Fresh barrels of air are sent down from the boat above.

Some animals, like water spiders, took their own supply of air (in a bubble) with them before people had thought of it. Early inventors also tried to do it.

In 3.9 you worked out how much air you breathed in a minute.

- Work out how many litres of air the three people would need to live under water for 3 minutes.
- Suppose you have a diving bell as big as your classroom. Work out how long the class will be able to stay under water.

You can breathe air more than once. So the air in the bell would last longer than you think. The next experiment will give you some idea how much longer.

How long can air last?

- Ask someone to hold a glass jar full of water over a trough also full of water.

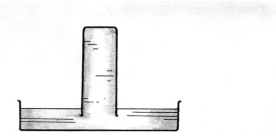

- Sterilise the end of a tube and breathe through it into the jar.

- Carefully put the gas jar over a lit candle.
- Time the candle until it goes out.

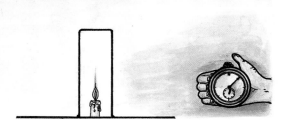

- Write your result in your notebook.

- Start again with a gas jar full of water over a trough.
- Breathe out into the jar, then breathe this air in and out again.
- Time how long the candle burns in the jar.
- Repeat this, re-using the air until the candle will not burn.
- Put your results in a table:

Number of times air was breathed	How long candle burned
1	
2	
3	

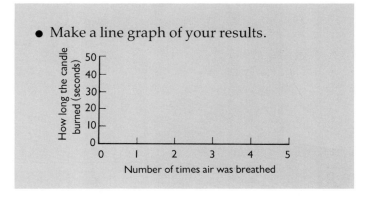

- Make a line graph of your results.

1 How long did the air last before the candle would not burn in it?

2 How long do you think the air in a diving bell would last?

3 How do modern divers and submarines solve this problem?

EXTRAS

1 Make a Cartesian diver. Use a Biro top with a paper clip on the open end as a diver, and a milk bottle full to the brim of water as the sea.

Half-fill the Biro top with water so that it just floats in water. Put it carefully into the milk bottle. Then press on the top of the bottle with the palm of your hand.

When you push on the water in the bottle, you are increasing the pressure in the water. What will this do to the air in the Biro top? Can you explain why the 'diver' dives?

2 One problem for humans going under water is depth. As you go deeper, the pressure gets greater. The pressure forces more air into your blood.

If a diver comes up too quickly, this compressed air cannot get out through the lungs. It forms air bubbles in the blood vessels. This is called 'the bends' and is very dangerous.

There are several solutions to this. Can you think of any?

3 Next time you take the top off a bottle of fizzy drink, watch carefully. Can you describe and explain what happens? The diver's 'bends' is another example of the same thing.

71

3·12 Investigating flight

Flying has always fascinated us.   *An 1807 design for a flying machine (seen from the front and from above)*

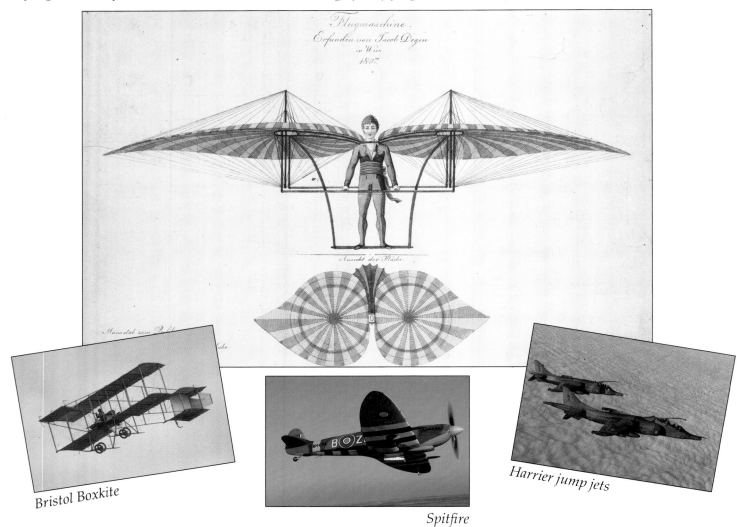

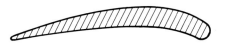
Bristol Boxkite

Spitfire

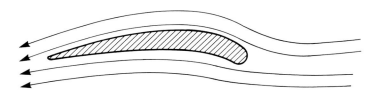
Harrier jump jets

How do aircraft fly?

Look carefully at the wings of the Spitfire in the photo. Imagine them cut through from front to back, like this:

This is called an aerofoil. It uses air to make an upward force called 'lift'. To make enough force to fly, the aerofoil has to move forwards through the air. The speed depends on the design, but in small aircraft it is about 100 km/hour. Propellers or jets are used to give enough forward speed.

Lift is produced by the way that the air moves over the aerofoil.

1 Which air travels further, the air going over, or the air going under the wing? You can measure the lines in the diagram if you are not sure.

The air going over the wing is 'stretched out'. This means that the air pressure is *lower* on top of the wing. Below the wing the pressure is *higher*. This difference makes the wing move up.

Making an aerofoil

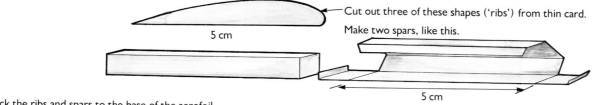

Cut out three of these shapes ('ribs') from thin card.

5 cm

Make two spars, like this.

5 cm

Stick the ribs and spars to the base of the aerofoil.

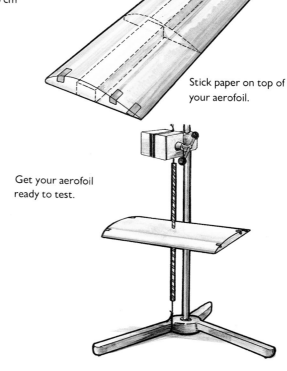

5 cm

10 cm

Stick paper on top of your aerofoil.

Get your aerofoil ready to test.

Testing your aerofoil

- Find the centre of gravity of your aerofoil. This is the point on which it will balance.
- Push a straw carefully through this point.
- Thread cotton through the straw and fix it tightly.
- Test your aerofoil by blowing towards its front ('leading') edge. It should lift.
- How does your aerofoil's lift compare with other groups'?

Flying machines

- Here are some ideas about how to make a fuselage to which you can fit your aerofoil.

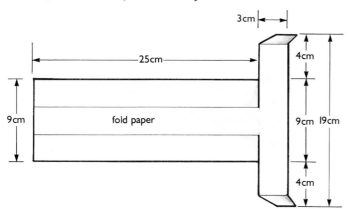

3cm

25cm

4cm

9cm

fold paper

9cm 19cm

4cm

Find the balance point. Glue the wing on top so that the balance point stays the same.

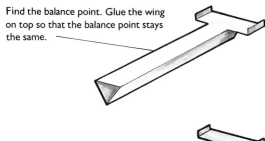

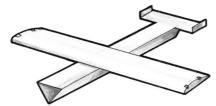

Investigating

- Have a competition with others in your class to see who can make the aircraft which will go furthest. You will need to use the best aerofoil you can.
- Find out how the plane's performance changes if you alter:
  - the length of the wings
  - the shape of the aerofoil
  - the length of the tail
  - the shape of the tail

  Only change one thing at a time! (Why?)

4·1 Using materials

Observing

- Cut a piece of paper into many small pieces. With your friends write on each piece of paper the name of a different object shown above.

- Now your group has to sort the things out. Try to sort them into three or four sets so that all the objects in one set have something in common.

- Make a poster of your group's results. Take one of your sets of paper names. Stick them all near each other on the poster. Put a title for the set on the poster. Do this for each of your sets.
- Be prepared to explain to another group why you have chosen the sets that you have.
- If you have time, make lists in your book of:
  – all the man-made materials in the display.
  – all the liquids in the display, and
  – all the gases in the display.

A materials machine

Some everyday materials
a balloon filled with air
50g of sand (9 points)
30 pins (4 points)
30 paper straws (6 points)
1 metre of string (2 points)
a 10cm strip of aluminium foil (7 points)
a little PVA wood glue (1 point)
$100cm^3$ plastic beaker (5 points)
2 yoghurt pots (8 points)
an elastic band (3 points)

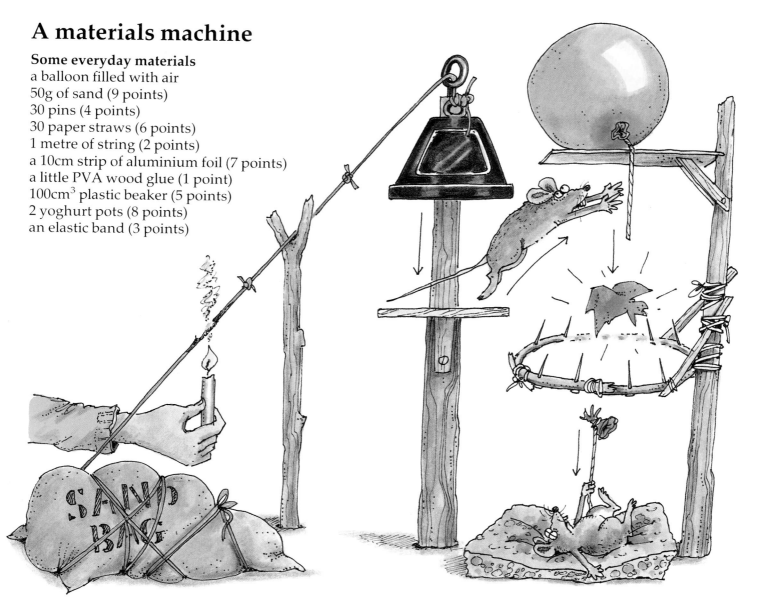

- Your group has to make a machine from these materials. It does not need to be as clever as the one in the cartoon! The machine has to use as many of the materials as possible to pop the balloon. You get the points shown on the list for using each item. To gain the points, you must use each item sensibly. But you will not get the points if you just use the item to decorate your machine!

- When you have made your machine (and tested it, of course), copy this table into your book and fill it in:

20/3/98 What I used in my materials machine			
Material	Used for	Because	Points

EXTRAS

1 Look in a shop or supermarket at the ways that food is packaged. Write a report on the different methods that you find. Say what materials are used, and try to explain why each is suitable for packaging food.

2 Make a list of the materials used to make a bicycle. For each one try to say where it is used and why it is used for that particular job. Your first one could be:
Steel   Used in the frame, because it is strong.

4·2 What a gas!

Gases and their uses

Gases are all around you, even though you cannot see them. Here are some important gases:

Hydrogen is very light. It explodes with air and is used as a fuel in rockets.

Ammonia is used to make fertilisers, textiles and explosives. There would be much less food in the world if we did not have ammonia.

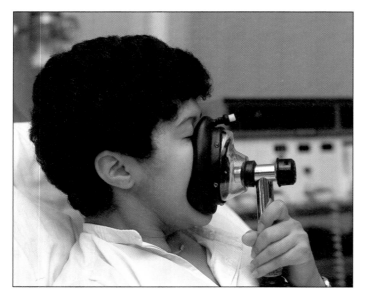

Oxygen is the gas of life. All animals need oxygen to stay alive. It is also used to help things burn: in welding torches and in rocket engines.

Natural gas is made from animals that died and then rotted millions of years ago. It is trapped under the rocks. Because it burns well, it makes a good fuel. In mines it is called firedamp because it can cause explosions.

Argon is a gas that is hard to change into anything else. It is unreactive. Argon is used to fill light bulbs. Because it is so unreactive, it stops the wire filament in the bulb from burning out.

Carbon dioxide is the fizz in fizzy drinks. This gas is also made when things burn. Too much carbon dioxide stops a fire altogether. Plants turn carbon dioxide into food called carbohydrate.

- Discuss with others in your group what the word GAS means. Write down how your group would explain the word to someone at junior school.
- Make a list of the gases that you know. You can start with the six on this page, but there are many others. If you can, say what each gas does, or where it is found.

What makes gases useful?

Gases are useful because they are squashy.

Gases can be pumped.

1 What would happen if air could not get past the washer?

2 The first bicycles had solid tyres. Why are modern bikes different? (Think how a solid ball compares with a balloon.)

3 Imagine your bicycle tyres were filled with water. What would it be like to ride?

Gases can be compressed for storing.

4 Compressed means squashed up. Why is the gas more useful squashed up like this?

5 Which other gases are stored squashed up?

Gases can be compressed to do work.

6 What other jobs do we use compressed gas for?

Observing

Gases expand when they are warm.

Expand means to spread out. Try this experiment:

- Get a flask with a narrow tube in the top.
- Run cold water over the outside to cool it.
- Hold the flask upside-down in both hands so that the narrow tube dips into some water. Watch carefully for a minute.
- Now hold the flask in two fingers at its neck. Keep the tube under water and watch.
- Write the experiment up in your book and explain what you saw.

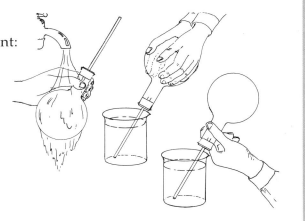

EXTRAS

1 An automatic supermarket door uses compressed air.

(**a**) When does the door open?

(**b**) How does it know when to open?

(**c**) How does it know when to close?

(**d**) How does the designer stop people getting hurt in the door?

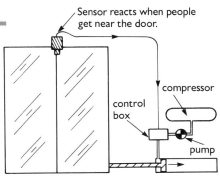

Sensor reacts when people get near the door.

compressor

control box

pump

Piston opens the door.

(**e**) Why doesn't the compressed air run out?

2 Most Underground trains have pneumatic doors. Pneumatic means powered by air. How is the control of a train door different from the control of a supermarket door? Why is there a difference?

4·3 Drip . . . Drip . . . Drip . . .

Liquids

- With a friend, write down a list of jobs that liquids do. Here is a starter:
  They are used for drinking.

Communicating

- Imagine that you are the editor of *Lovely Liquids*. This is a paper that is sent out to primary schools to explain liquids to children. Design and make a front page for the paper that has information and ideas about liquids on it. It must appeal to young children, and be easy for them to look at and read.

A liquid game

Now try a game with your friend.
- You have to think of a word that describes a liquid, e.g. runny.
- Then your friend must try to think of a non-liquid that the word also describes, e.g. sand.
- If your friend can think of a non-liquid, then he/she gets a point. If he/she can't, you do. You may need an umpire!
- Take it in turns to go first. Write down any words that you think of which only describe liquids.
- When you have both had ten turns of going first, put some liquid words in your book.

When is a liquid not a liquid?

It is sometimes difficult to decide when a liquid becomes a solid. You may have trouble deciding in the experiment below.

Starch is used to make sauces (like custard or gravy) thick . . . and sometimes lumpy!

Starch particles are long and thin. When they are warmed with water, the starch absorbs the water. The particles get bigger, and they link together.

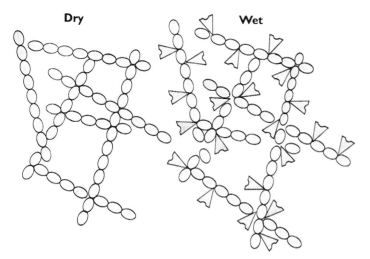

Your group has to find out how long it takes for gravy to become a solid at different temperatures.

A suitable mixture to use is 5g of starch (ordinary wallpaper paste or cornflour will do) in 50cm³ of water.

You could try these temperatures: 20°C, 30°C, 40°C, 50°C.

- Before starting you must decide:
  - What are you going to alter each time?
  - How will you alter it?
  - How will you decide when the starch is a solid. (Hint: Looking is not a fair test. A runniness meter will be needed. You can make a runniness meter by measuring how fast the liquid runs down a slope.)
  - What will you keep the same in each test?

  You must put the answers to these questions in your book before you start.

- Carry out the experiment.
- When you have finished, write up your results.
- Find out if other groups' results agree with yours. If they are different, try to explain why.

   water molecule

⬭⬭⬭   starch molecule

1. Water molecules break up a ball of starch molecules. The ones trapped in the middle can now get out.
2. Water molecules are attracted to the starch molecules. The starch molecules are attracted to each other.

EXTRAS

Why do engines need oil?

Oil does many jobs in an engine. Its main task is to stop the moving parts from rubbing on each other. This job is called lubrication. Oil also:

- absorbs particles which can cause wear
- spreads heat out
- seals tiny gaps
- reduces noise.

Oil is a mixture of liquids that do these jobs.

1 What has to be oiled in your house to keep it moving?

2 Which parts of a bike should be oiled regularly?

3 What happens to the bike if it is not oiled?

4·4 Solids

- Test at least ten solids in your laboratory.
- Write down a list of words that describes each solid. The sort of words to use are:

| Hard | Strong | Bendy | Stretchy | Warm |
| Heavy | Waterproof | Smooth | See-through | |

Here is an example:

27/3/98   Testing some solids

Plastic ruler: hard, white, bendy, light, tough, waterproof, smooth, sinks.

Polythene bag: ...

- Look through all the words you have used to describe solids. Write down the ten words that you have used most. Are there any words that describe *all* solids?
- Write down ten words that describe most liquids (look back at your work on the last page).
- Write down ten words that would describe most gases.
- Discuss with your group why a solid is different from a liquid or a gas. Write down the most important difference you can find.
- Find out which groups have said something else. Whose answer is best?

Information about solids

Solids are made of particles held firmly in place. The particles are so small that a pencil contains about 300 000 million million million of them.

If you try to squash a solid, the tiny particles push apart to stop you. If you try to stretch it, they pull together to stop you. These pushes and pulls give solids a fixed shape. The shape is only changed if you push, pull or twist hard enough.

Is a rubber glove solid?

This is how a rubber glove is made:

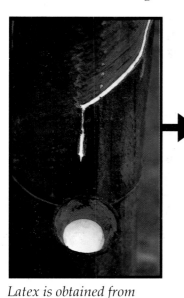

Latex is obtained from rubber trees in Malaysia.

The milky liquid is brought to a factory in the UK.

Chemicals are added. The rubber mixture is heated, then cooled, to make it just right.

Hand shapes are dipped in the rubber mixture. Thin layers of rubber become solid on the shapes.

The gloves are rinsed and taken off the hand shapes.

- Make a written flowchart of this process. Your first box could be:

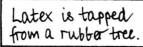
Latex is tapped from a rubber tree. →

- Write a list of words that describe a rubber glove.

1 What is it about the glove that makes it a SOLID?

2 When it was made, at what stage did it become solid?

Choosing a material

- You have to decide what sort of material you would use for the jobs shown. You only have to write down some words to describe the material. You do not need to name it.

Job 1: Tooth fillings.   Job 2: Hairdrier casing.   Job 3: String for doing up parcels.   Job 4: Toilet paper.

EXTRAS

1 Design your own torch.
(**a**) Decide what materials you would use for: the electrical parts, the casing, the lens, and the switch.

(**b**) Why would you choose these materials?

2 What does the material that a brake block is made of need to be like? How would you like to improve on the rubber blocks used on most bikes now? (See the picture in 1.9.)

Houses

Throughout the world, people use natural materials to build houses.

Try to answer these questions about each house:
1. What part of the world is it from?
2. What material is it made from?
3. Why is it made from this material?
4. What are the disadvantages of this material?

Using stone

In Britain, many houses are made from stone. Here are four types of stone that are often used:

Limestone from the West Midlands

Slate from North Wales

Sandstone from Dorset

Granite from Cumbria

- Test samples of each of the rocks. Try to compare:
  - How easy they are to scratch.
  - How heavy pieces of the same size are.
  - How waterproof they are.
  - What happens when you rub them.
  - If they break and, how they break.

Look carefully at the photo of each rock.

5 Are all the rocks made of grains?
6 Which has the biggest grains?
7 Which of the rocks would be easiest to build with? Why?
8 Which rock would wear away quickest?

Most buildings in Britain are made of brick or concrete. These materials are cheap and easy to make.

Concrete

Concrete is a mixture of four things:
- cement (from limestone and clay)
- sand
- gravel
- water

Making a strong mixture
- Find out how much cement, sand, gravel and water is needed to make strong concrete. For a fair test, each piece of concrete that you make must be the same size. 10cm long and 1cm square is quite big enough.
- Make the pieces with different amounts of each of the materials. Put them in moulds and let them set. Take care not to get concrete on your hands, or throw waste concrete down the sink. (Why?)

Testing the concrete
- Make up a good and fair test for your concrete beams. Have a good look at them for weaknesses before you destroy them! Be careful of falling weights.

- Write up carefully everything you have done. Include:
  - a title
  - the mixtures you used
  - the tests you did
  - the results you got
  - what you decided.

EXTRAS

1 Here is some information about the amount of concrete used in Britain.

2 Find out how concrete is made even stronger when it is used in bridges or tall buildings.

Year	1945	1950	1955	1960	1965	1970	1975	1980	1985
Amount of cement used (million tons)	4.1	9.9	12.7	13.5	17.2	17.2	16.9	14.8	12.6

(a) Make a bar chart that shows how much concrete has been used in each year since 1945.
(b) What shape is the bar chart?
(c) What does the shape tell you?

4·6 *Making things stronger*

Bridges

The strength of a bridge depends on the material it is made from and how the material is used.

Tarr Steps, a prehistoric bridge on Exmoor

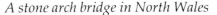
A stone arch bridge in North Wales

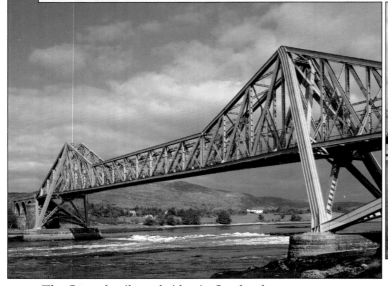

The Connel railway bridge in Scotland

The Severn Bridge near Bristol

Stone is strong, but a single-stone bridge cannot be very large. It also has to be very thick. Why?

Arch bridges are also made of stone, but the stones are arranged in a special way. A stone arch can be stronger and longer than a single stone.

A single piece of metal is not very long. But if many pieces are joined in the right way, a long and strong bridge is possible.

A suspension bridge uses wire cables hung from strong towers. This can be used to span very long gaps.

Compression and tension

Most parts of a bridge are under pressure. Some are being squashed. This is called

➡️ COMPRESSION ⬅️

Others are being stretched. This is called

⬅️ TENSION ➡️

- Make a bridge from a spill or a twig.
- Use your fingers as a heavy load and push on the middle of the bridge.

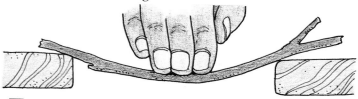

1 Where is the twig being compressed?
2 Where is it being stretched?

- If you press hard enough, the twig will split open at the tension point. It will also look all squashed up at the compression point. Try it.
- Draw the damaged twig very carefully. Label the compression and tension points.
- Look at the photo of the arch bridge. Draw a sketch of it in your notebook.
- Imagine there is a heavy load on it. Colour in blue the parts of the bridge that are being compressed.

3 What stops the bridge from falling down?

- Look at the photo of the suspension bridge. Make a sketch of it in your notebook.
- Use blue to mark in the parts that are compressed. Use red to mark the parts that are in tension.

A model bridge

Bridge engineers use scale models to test their ideas.
- Use straws, card, string and glue to make a scale model of the Severn Bridge.

Investigating

- Plan an investigation to find out how much your bridge sags when different loads are put on it. Decide what you will measure and how you will measure it.

How will you alter the load?
- Carry out the investigation, and write up what you find out.
- Find ways to make your design stronger.

Shaping a stronger bridge

- You have to plan an experiment to find out how strong different shapes of card are. You could try flat, doubled, corrugated, round, square, and any others.

  The experiment must be fair! What will you do to make sure it is?

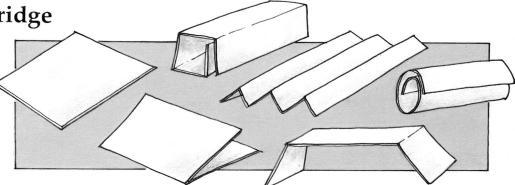

A bridge competition

Your class has to make the strongest possible bridge from one single sheet (290mm × 210mm) of card and 200mm of Sellotape.

- The bridge has to span a gap of 25cm.
- The bridge must be at least 5cm wide.

- It must not touch the ground between the edges.
- Design and make the best bridge you can.
- You can test each group's bridge and see who has made the strongest one. Be careful of falling weights.

EXTRAS

1 Make a sketch of a bridge near your home. What is the bridge made of?

2 Colour in blue the parts being compressed.

3 Colour in red the parts being stretched (in tension).

4·7 Design a stool

Laboratory stools

Look at the stools in your science laboratory. Are they the same as the stools in the pictures?

- With your friends, make a list of things you think are important in a laboratory stool. You should be able to put at least ten things down.

1 What would be the single most important thing about a laboratory stool for each of these people:
  - you?
  - your science teacher?
  - your headteacher?
  - your parents?
  - the firm that makes the stools?
  - the people who work for that firm?

Keeping it stable

One thing you may have on your list is how well the stool stands up (how stable it is).

- Make some model stools with straws for legs and Plasticine seats. Try different numbers of legs, and fix them at different angles. Make them so the seats are all the same height off the ground.

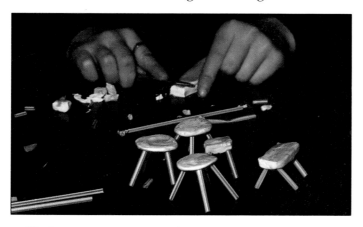

- Find a way to compare how easily the stools can be tipped over. Make sure your test is fair. Try to find an accurate way to measure the results (just pushing with a finger is not very scientific!).

Here is some equipment that might be useful:

Newton meters (0–1N and 0–10N). These measure pulls.

Cotton or string   Card
10 × 10g masses   Scissors
Blu-Tack   Glue

- Write a report of your findings.

2 Are the stools in *your* laboratory the most stable shape?

Costing it out

Imagine your straw stool is a real design. Imagine that straws cost 10p per millimetre, and that Plasticine costs 10p per gram.

You have to make a stool with these specifications:
– a Plasticine seat (at least 30mm long, 20mm wide and 5mm thick). It may be any shape – round, square, triangular . . .

– 45mm off the ground
– stable
– cheap

● Design and make a stool that meets these requirements.
● Work out its cost.
● Make a note of any other good features that it has.
● Compare your design with others made by your class. Which is best?

Choosing a design

3 Look at the information about stools. If you were the Head of the Science Department, which type would you choose? Why?

EXTRAS

1 Why are stools not made wider at the base?

2 (a) Here are six different glasses. Put them in order of stability, with the most stable first. Explain how you decided on your order.

(b) Why do people buy the least stable glasses?

3 (a) Choose an object that you use every day. Make a list of things that are wrong or annoying about it.
(b) Make a list of ways to improve the object.
(c) Do a design for a new object that gets round all the things that you dislike. Why is it not made like that?

4·8 *Plastics everywhere*

Testing plastics

Although plastics have only been around for 50 years, they are very important. You can test the differences between some of these items in the experiment below.

● For each plastic that you test, you should write down this information:

Object tested:

What it looks like:

What it feels like:

What happens when it is pulled:

What happens when it is cut:

Does it float?

Does it bend when it is warm?

(Take great care not to melt the plastics. The fumes are poisonous, and molten plastic can burn you, or damage the bench.)

● Test at least five different plastics.
● Then use a key to identify the plastics if you can. Not all plastics are on this key, so be careful! There are many other types of plastic; if you have any odd bits at home, you can bring them and test them.
● You may have found some plastics that are not in the key. If so, make a new key in your book that covers all the plastics that you have tested.

What plastics are

Plastics are made from natural substances. The most important one is oil, but other chemicals, like chlorine (which comes from salt), are also used.

This is how many plastics are made:

Crude oil is a mixture of liquids. A refinery separates these liquids from each other.

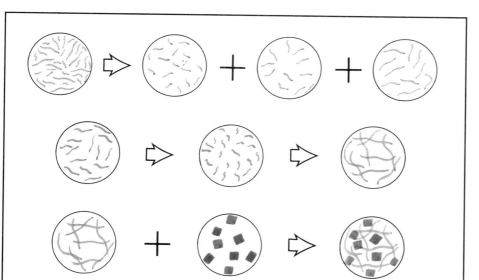

Naphtha is used to make plastics. The molecules of naphtha are broken up and then joined again to make long chains. These are called polymers.

The new plastic is squeezed into shape.

Chemicals are added to give colour and stiffness.

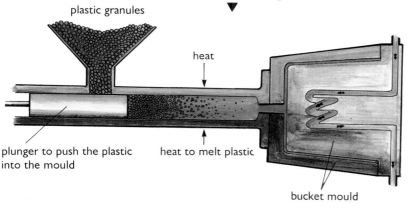

plastic granules

heat

cold water to make the plastic solid again

plunger to push the plastic into the mould

heat to melt plastic

bucket mould

Communicating

- Write to a younger sister or brother explaining how a drop of oil is made into a plastic bucket. Use the pictures to help you.

1 Make a list of reasons why most buckets are now made of plastic instead of metal.

2 Are there any problems with plastics?

3 Why do the chemicals in oil have to be sorted out before they can be made into plastics?

4 Why are plastics called polymers?

EXTRAS

1 (a) You have to find a plastic that can be used for wrapping food. What should the plastic be like? Make a list of your ideas.
(b) Look in a local shop at food wrappings. Make a table that shows the foods you see, and what they are wrapped in.

2 A Biro consists of several different plastics. Do a large drawing of a Biro, showing the inside as well as the outside. Put labels on your drawing that show the type of plastic used for each job.

3 What plastic materials have you used today? Make a list.

4·9 Fibres and fabrics

Fibres into fabric

Fibres are thin, single strands. Natural fibres like flax, hair and wool have been used for thousands of years to make clothes. Nowadays synthetic fibres are also used. Apart from clothes, they are made into many useful things.

These objects are all made from fibres.

A statue about 5000 years old, from the Middle East, showing a man wearing a woven garment

ONLY £2.99

1 What do you think the fibre used for each object should be like? One example is done for you:

Trousers: The fibre should be hard-wearing, bendy, soft to touch, easy to weave.

A yarn is made from a lot of fibres. Fibres can be made into a yarn by spinning.

● Make and try out a small hand spinner.

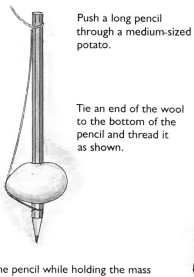

Push a long pencil through a medium-sized potato.

Tie an end of the wool to the bottom of the pencil and thread it as shown.

Now spin the pencil while holding the mass of wool. Feed in the wool as it spins.

When the length of wool is spun, wind it around the pencil tip and then rethread as shown.

Is a yarn stronger than its fibres?

You can make a model of a yarn using newspaper.

- Cut a page of newspaper into 0.5cm-wide strips. These are your fibres.
- Think of a way of comparing the strength of the fibres before and after 'spinning'. You could try 20 paper fibres unspun, 20 spun (twisted) tightly together and 20 plaited together. Make sure your test is fair!!
- If you can get some wool from a fleece, you could try this experiment with real materials. It is more difficult, though. You can use your small hand spinner to make the yarn.

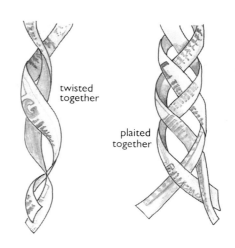

twisted together

plaited together

How a fabric is made

First, fibres are spun into a yarn. The yarn is then woven or knitted to make a fabric.

2 Why are woven fabrics usually stronger than knitted ones?

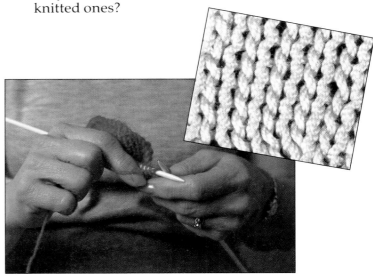

EXTRAS

1 Look at as many different types of fabric as you can. Use a hand lens or a microscope.
(a) List all the ways in which the fabrics look the same.
(b) Write down any differences. Are synthetic fibres (like nylon) different from natural fibres (like wool or cotton)?

2 Find a way of measuring the strength of a human hair. (The biggest problem is how to clamp the ends of the hair. A piece of rubber clamped on to the hair is one possible solution.)
(a) Are all hairs the same strength?
(b) Which colour is strongest?

3 Have a look at home at as many clothing labels as you can.
(a) Make a list of all the materials used in your clothes.
(b) Which is the most common? Are your clothes mainly natural or artificial fabrics?

4·10 Keeping warm

All these things are designed to keep animals warm. They all have something in common – spaces where air is trapped.

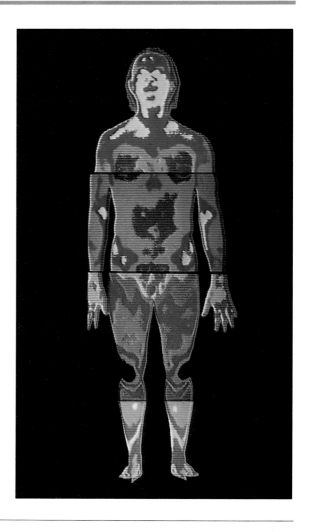

Look at this photo. It shows a thermal image of a person with no clothes on. The brighter the colour, the more heat the camera has found at that point.

1 Which areas of the body do you think produce most heat?
2 Why do you think some areas are hotter than others?

Comparing different heat insulators

A good heat insulator stops heat from escaping.

3 Which of these make the better insulator:
 – a string vest or a T-shirt?
 – a wet jumper or a dry one?
 – fabric or plastic bubbles?
 – feathers or fur?
 – two thin layers of insulation or one thick one?

● Design and carry out an experiment to decide on one of the insulators above. You can use any of this equipment:
 – a hot potato (70°C), with a hole in for a thermometer
 – a thermometer
 – insulation for your potato (you will have to decide exactly what insulation to use, and how to use it)
 – rubber bands

● You should aim to take the temperature of the potato every minute for at least 15 minutes.

● Do a graph of your results. If you test two insulators, put the results on the same graph, but in different colours.

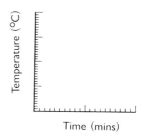

● Work out the fall in temperature in 15 minutes.
● Make a table for all the insulators tested. Show the fall in temperature of the potato for each one.
● Which is the best insulator? What makes it better than the others?

Size and insulation

- If you have time, try using two potatoes of different sizes. Put exactly the same insulation on each potato, then find out how quickly they cool.

4 What do your results tell you about how much insulation a baby needs compared to an adult?

Scott and Amundsen

In 1911 both Captain Scott and Roald Amundsen tried to lead teams of men to the South Pole. Amundsen got there first, and got back safely. Scott got very near, but mistook one of Amundsen's marker flags for the South Pole. He, and several of his team, died on the return journey.

The two teams used different clothing. Scott had specially designed woollen clothes. Amundsen chose what Eskimos wear: reindeer fur. Reindeer fur is made of millions of hollow hairs. This makes the fur very good at trapping air, and also very light.

Amundsen said: 'The inner and outer anorak hang lightly outside the trousers and the air has free access all the way up the body. Inner and outer trousers are held up round the waist with a cord and hang free over the boots so that air can circulate freely. I find it excellent, and the only way to wear fur clothes if one is to avoid sweating.'

The men on the polar expeditions had to work hard pulling sledges and controlling their animals. This made them sweat. When they stopped working, they would have cooled down fast. This could have been dangerous.

5 Why is sweating dangerous in cold conditions?
6 How was Amundsen's clothing better than Scott's?
7 Why do you think this helped him to reach the South Pole first?

- Write a letter to Scott before he leaves Britain, telling him the sort of equipment to take.

Modern ways to keep warm

Modern mountaineers and explorers look like this: This equipment is designed to trap air in the clothing, and to stop this air from moving.

Air is a good insulator if it stays in one place. Look back at the thermal image pictures on the other page.

8 Which parts of the body let out most heat? Which parts of the body does the mountaineer have most clothes on?

socks, inner felt boots, outer leather boots

EXTRAS

1 Why do you think duck feathers are used in the best sleeping bags?

2 A string vest or thermal underwear on its own is not very warm. Why not? What do you need as well?

3 If you get cold, what does your body do to warm you up?

4 Why is double glazing a good insulator? What other ways are there of insulating a house?

First layer: thermal underwear; second layer: fibre-filled jacket and pants; third layer: fibre-filled jacket and pants.

4·11 *Investigating hot-air balloons*

Early balloons

People have always wanted to fly, but it was not possible before 1783. In that year, the Montgolfier brothers found that a paper bag filled with hot air would lift off the ground.

They made a cloth balloon 11 metres in diameter (about the length of your science laboratory). The balloon was filled with smoke from a fire. It took off successfully.

The Montgolfiers did not understand why the balloon worked. They knew it was something to do with the fire, but they thought it might be the *smoke* that made it rise.

● Can you think of a way of showing them that it was heat rather than smoke that gave the balloon lift?

This first balloon flight was followed by other longer and higher manned flights.

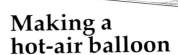

Modern balloons

Modern balloons are made of nylon and are very big. They can be over 50 metres from top to bottom. A propane gas burner is used to heat the air in the balloon.

When it is in the air, the balloon is at the mercy of the elements. It can only go the way that the air currents are going.

Balloonists are keen observers of flags and chimney smoke. These things show where there are helpful air currents.

1 There are two ways of getting a balloon back to the ground again without damage. What do you think they are?

Making a hot-air balloon

Opposite there is a design for a small balloon your group can make. You will need:
- some light material (tissue paper, thin plastic etc.)
- scissors
- glue or sticky tape
- paper clips

Choosing a material
● Decide what properties your balloon material needs to have.
● Think about how you are going to join the sections together.
● Try out small sections of the material you choose before making the whole balloon. Take care! This is not easy.

Balancing your balloon
● If the balloon is not stable, it will tip over when it is ready for take-off. To stop this, the bottom needs to be slightly heavier than the rest. Find a way of doing this.

1. Cut six pieces of material.

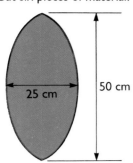

25 cm 50 cm

2. Join the pieces like this:

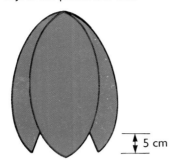

5 cm

Leave the last 5 cm unglued.

3. Fold the ends under, and glue them.

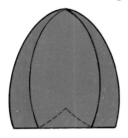

4. Balance your balloon with paper clips.

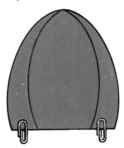

Take-off!

You will not be able to fly your balloon outside on a windy day. You may be able to test it inside in a hall or gym, but only if you are very sensible.

Warming the air in the balloon is the most difficult job. You must be sure that you will not damage the material. Worse still, you could have a fire. **Take care**.

Here is one way to warm the air:

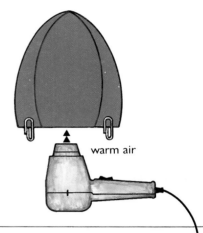

warm air

Comparing the balloons

- After some testing, you should be able to compare your balloon with other groups' balloons. You can do this by comparing how long each balloon will fly for.
- For each balloon that takes part, write down the results like this:

31/3/98 Comparing balloons			
Whose balloon?	Material used	Joints made of	Time of flight
Nasrin and Joe	Paper	Glue	15 seconds

- Write a report of the testing and what it told you.
- If you have time, try to make an improved design. If you decorate your balloon (without making it too heavy), it will look very impressive.

EXTRAS

1 Why is nylon used instead of cloth in modern balloons?

2 Why do you think most balloons use hot air instead of a very light gas (like hydrogen)?

3 What do you think is the most dangerous point in a balloon flight? What dangers would you look out for?

4 Explain why a balloon flies to someone who has never seen a balloon before.

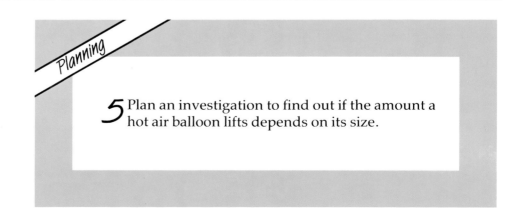

Planning

5 Plan an investigation to find out if the amount a hot air balloon lifts depends on its size.

5 LIFE

This unit is different from the others. Each topic usually takes up one page, not two. An asterisk (*) in the text means there is something about that organism in the reference section at the back. After the reference section there is a glossary. This explains some of the harder words in this unit.

5·1 Dead or alive?

This bear is alive . . .   . . . but this one isn't.

● Discuss with your friends all the differences between a real bear and a toy bear.

A life test

● Between you, make a list of questions that will test if something is alive or not. Your questions should have 'YES' answers if the object you are looking at is alive.

  Your first question might be: 'Does it move?'

● Try your life test on these things:
  – a rose   – a robot
  – a candle   – yeast*
  – a tree-stump

  Change your questions if they are not quite right.

● When you have a complete list, put a date and title in your book, and copy down your group's list of questions.

● Read about amoebae* and algae* in the reference section, then try your test on them. Does it work?

Where did it all start?

No one is sure how life began.

One theory is that the Earth was a piece of hot rock thrown out from an exploding star. As this rock cooled, the atmosphere formed. Violent storms and lightning made some of the gases in the atmosphere join together. The new chemicals were similar to the chemicals in living things.

The first living things were probably tiny water plants – rather like algae. These plants made oxygen and changed the atmosphere. As time went on, the plants became bigger and more complicated. Eventually, simple animals developed. You can see some of this process on an evolution chart in 5.13.

EXTRAS

1 Look through the reference section on pages 136 to 141. Which is the simplest living thing there? Explain your choice.

2 Which is the most complicated living thing in the reference section? Explain your choice. How is your simplest organism *like* your most complicated one?

5·2 Sorting out living things

Living things are called organisms. Organisms can be divided into two types: animals and plants. The main difference between them is that plants can make their own food. Also, plants cannot move as far or as fast as most animals.

- Look through the organisms in the reference section. Make a list of all the plants. What features do they have in common?

- Imagine that you have to explain the difference between an animal and a plant to your parents. Write them a few sentences that explain the differences. You can use an animal and a plant from the reference section as examples if you want.

Observing

Sorting organisms into groups

Living things can be sorted into groups so that each group contains organisms that are similar. Your group will need some small pieces of paper and a large one to display them on.

- Cut out about thirty small pieces of paper. On each one, write the name of an organism from pages 136–141.

- Look carefully at the photographs on pages 136–141, then sort the pieces of paper into groups. You can decide what a group is. For example, you could put all the plants in one group. Try to use between four and eight groups.

Now look at the groups on pages 134–5.

- Turn the display paper sideways, and copy the classification tree, with the headings, on to it.

- Then try to place all your pieces of paper under the right headings. The information in the reference section should help you. Stick them down when you all agree they are right.

EXTRAS

1 Your teacher is leading an expedition to the Amazon jungle. The expedition has discovered the remains of an animal that they cannot identify. It seems to have a backbone, but they need your help to classify it.

Your group are the expedition's scientific advisers. You have a poor radio link to the explorers. Decide on THREE questions that will tell you what type of vertebrate the animal is. As the radio link may fail, you must put the questions in order of importance. The group that can classify the animal correctly with fewest questions wins.

2 Which groups do the organisms below fit into? Explain your choices.

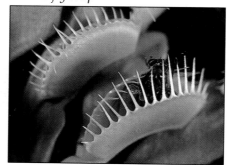

Sunflower
Venus fly trap

Stick insect
Sea anemone

5·3 Cells

All living things are made of cells. In some animals, the whole animal is a cell. This cell has to do everything: move, feed, reproduce . . .

Most organisms are made of many different cells. Each type of cell has a different job. Some are joined together in large groups called a tissue.

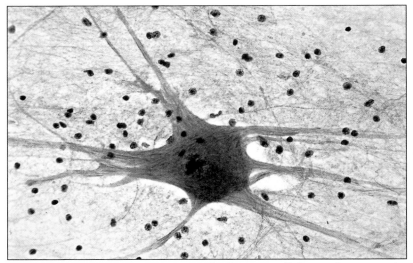

▲ *A nerve cell from a human spine*

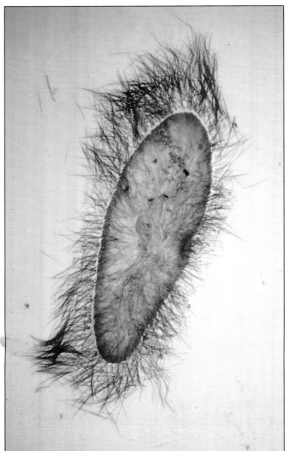

Paramecium: a single-cell organism

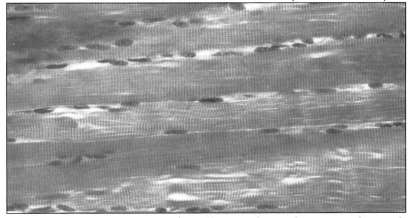

▲ *Cell tissue from a human neck muscle*

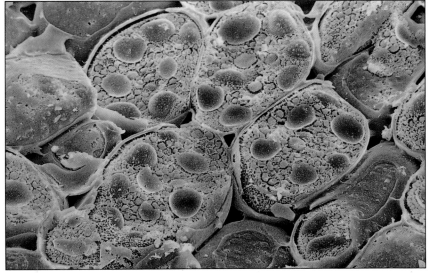

Cell tissue from a bean. The darker spots are grains of starch. The bean will use them as nourishment when it germinates

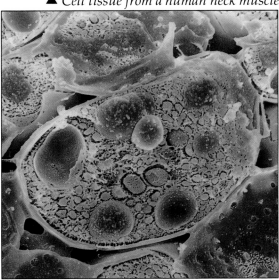

A single cell in a bean

Other cells are on their own. They have to be separate to do their job.

Red blood cells carry oxygen round your body. White blood cells help to fight disease.

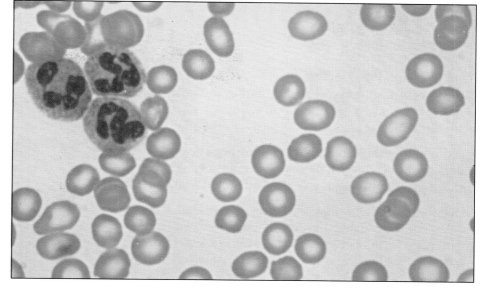

Three white cells among red cells in human blood

What is in a cell?

Most cells contain these parts: cell wall, cytoplasm and a nucleus.

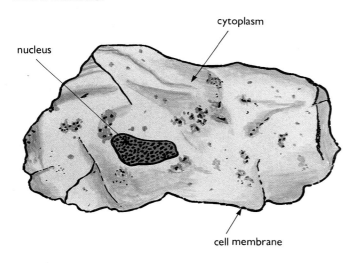

The cell wall or membrane holds the cell together. It can let chemicals, food and waste in and out of the cell.

The cytoplasm is where the cell makes and stores chemicals.

The nucleus controls what the cell does. It also contains the information that new cells are made from.

● Draw sketches of the cells on these pages. In each cell, label the parts that you can see.

Cells and their jobs

A cell's shape and design depends on its job.

Bean skin cells have thick walls to help protect the bean.

Red blood cells are thin and squashy so that they can get through tiny blood vessels while carrying oxygen around the body.

Most cells are so small that you must use a microscope to see them.

● Look at some cells under the microscope, then answer these questions.

1 Draw two or three cells of each type. Label the parts you know.
2 What jobs does the cell do?
3 Is the cell in a pattern with other cells or on its own?
4 How is the cell designed for its job?

EXTRAS

1 Answer questions 2–4 above for the cells that are shown in photos on these pages.

2 Find out about the amoeba* and some human cells (blood, muscle, brain). Answer questions 2–4 above for these cells.

5·4 New cells from old

Your cells are dying all the time. Every day about 200 thousand million of your red blood cells die. If you did not make new ones, you would have none at all after six weeks.

Your skin cells also die. You have about seven layers of skin cells which wear away. If new skin cells did not grow, your skin would very quickly disappear.

New cells develop from old ones. First of all, the nucleus of the old cell divides. Then a new cell membrane forms between the old nucleus and the new one. Finally, the cell divides. The new cell is an exact copy of the old one.

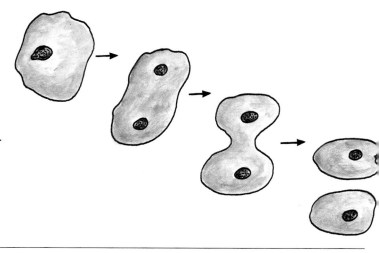

Yeast cells

- Read about yeast*. Make a note in your book that says:
  - what yeast is
  - how yeast cells develop
  - how yeast gets energy to grow and divide
  - what yeast is used for

How fast does yeast reproduce?
- Design and carry out an experiment that will tell you how much yeast is made from 1 gram of yeast in 24 hours. Think carefully!
  - What conditions will you keep the yeast in?
  - How will you measure the yeast at the end?

Investigating

What does yeast need to reproduce?
Books say that yeast cells need sugar, water and warmth to reproduce.
- Plan and carry out investigations to test if the books are right or not. It may help your planning to know that, when yeast reproduces, it makes bubbles of carbon dioxide.

Be very careful to decide what you will alter and what you will keep the same in each experiment. Try the experiment. You may need to work with other groups to test out all the different possibilities.

EXTRAS

1 The nucleus of a cell contains information about what the cell is like and how it works. The information is contained in thin strings called chromosomes. When a cell divides, the chromosomes in the cell have to be copied so that the new cell has a set of instructions. Use the reference section glossary to find out what a chromosome is like.

2 Look up yeast in a cookery book:
  (a) What is it used to make?
  (b) Why is it useful for cooking?
  (c) What else is yeast used for?

5·5 New plants

Taking cuttings

One way of making a new plant is to use part of an old plant. Gardeners take cuttings from a healthy plant to start a new one.

Plants grown this way are always identical to the parent plant. Can you explain why this is? Have a look back at cell division in 5.4 if you are not sure.

Making seeds

New plants also grow from seeds. A seed contains all the information that is needed for the new plant. Where does it come from?

Half of the information comes from special cells in a grain of pollen. The other half is from special cells in the ovule.

If a seed is to form, the pollen has to reach the ovule. When it does, the ovule develops into a seed.

If the pollen and ovule are from one plant, the new plant will be like a cutting, exactly the same as the parent. But if the pollen comes from a different plant, the new plant can be quite different from the parent.

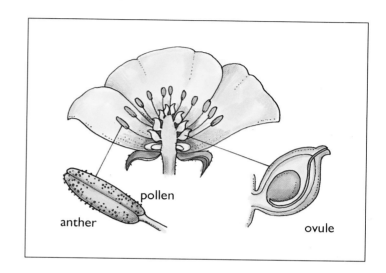

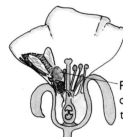
Pollen from the anthers of one plant collects on the hairs of a bee that is searching for nectar.

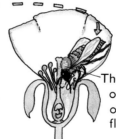
The pollen is brushed on to the stigma of a different flower.

A tube grows down from a pollen grain to the ovary.

The pollen travels down the tube and fertilises one ovule in the ovary.

What is inside a seed?

- Very carefully cut a broad bean seed lengthwise with a scalpel. Can you find the parts labelled here?

radicle (baby root)

testa (hard case)

plumule (baby shoot)

cotyledon (food store)

1 Most of the seed is an energy store. Why does the seed need such a large energy store?

EXTRAS

1 Read in the reference section about how algae, strawberries and mushrooms reproduce.
(**a**) Which of these three make new plants that are exactly the same as the parent?
(**b**) How are mushrooms different from the other two?

Planning

2 Use the reference section to find out what food mushrooms need. Imagine you are a farmer who grows mushrooms. Plan an experiment to find out on what material they will grow best.

5·6 Sowing seeds

Fertilised ovules become seeds. The ovary that contains the ovules swells. It becomes a fruit.

How do seeds spread?

Most plants try to spread their seeds as far as possible. This gives the species a greater chance of surviving and spreading.

● Imagine that you are a tree which needs to spread its seeds. Use a dried pea as a seed, and a piece of 290 × 210mm paper. Use the paper to make and test something that will carry the seed as far away as possible from you.

To test your seed spreader you must DROP it from 2 metres above the ground. You may not throw it. To get some ideas, read how different plants spread their seeds*.

Think carefully how to compare different designs. Is it fair to do just one test of each?

● When you have finished, compare your design with other groups. Write up your work.
● Is there a plant that uses the same sort of design as yours? Try to find out if you do not know.

Growing seeds

Seeds can survive for a long time without growing. But when conditions are right, they develop quickly. This is called germination.

Planning

What conditions do beans need to germinate?
● Plan an experiment to find out which of these things a bean needs:
   – warmth   – water
   – light   – soil

● If you can, try out your experiment. Different groups may need to try out different conditions.

EXTRAS

1 Make a list of the methods that plants use to spread their seeds. (Look up flower, fir, strawberry, sycamore, wheat in the reference section.)

2 Which of the foods that you eat are really fruits with seeds in them? Where are the seeds? What do you usually call them?

3 (a) Germinate a seed on some blotting paper. Water it and look at it carefully each day. Measure the length of the root and the shoot each day.

(b) Use your measurements to make a line graph (height up the side, days along the bottom) that shows how the root and the shoot grow. Does the root or the shoot grow first? Which is the longer?

5.7 New animals

Communicating

Some animals can make new animals without a male and a female.

● Read about amoebae* and aphids*. Write a brief summary that will remind you how these two animals reproduce.

● Can you think of some reasons why they reproduce like this?

Eggs and sperms

Most animals need a male and a female to make a new individual. The new animal contains some information from the father and some from the mother. This means that the new animal will not be identical to its parents.

The parents carry this information in special cells: the mother has egg cells and the father has sperm cells. These cells are very small, but they contain all the information needed to make a new animal. You started life from an egg about the size of a full stop, and a sperm 20 times smaller.

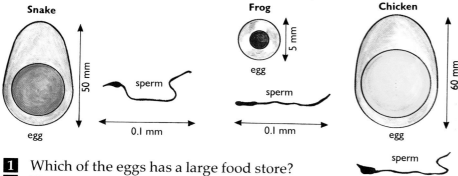

Snake 50 mm egg sperm 0.1 mm
Frog 5 mm egg sperm 0.1 mm
Chicken 60 mm egg sperm 0.1 mm

1 Which of the eggs has a large food store?
2 How will the eggs with little food get more?
3 (a) How big is the chicken sperm?
 (b) The information to make the new chicken is carried in chromosomes in the head of the sperm. How big is this? Could this develop into a new chicken on its own?
4 Is the egg from one species of animal always bigger than its sperm?
5 What do all the sperms have in common?
6 Has the size of the egg or sperm got anything to do with the size of the adult animal? Explain your answer.

A new individual

1 A male has to find a female.

2 A sperm from the male has to reach an egg from the female.

3 The egg has to be fertilised.

4 The new individual has to develop.

5 The new individual has to become an adult.

EXTRAS

Find out how one animal reproduces. You should be able to discover something about each of the stages 1–5 above, and how long it takes. Each person in your group should read about a different animal. When you have found out all you can, explain your research to the rest of your group.

Choose from these animals: elephants*, cod*, snakes*, woodlice*, chickens*, frogs*, slugs*, tapeworms*, starfish*, spiders*.

5·8 New humans 1 – a love story

Humans are very special animals. They spend longer bringing up their young and looking after them than any other species. They are also the only species that can decide *when* to have children. It is an important decision. Children take a lot of looking after.

Humans reproduce like other animals. First, a man or woman needs to find someone who will be special for them. Unlike most animals, humans usually pair up for life, so it is important to find the right person. This is really what we mean by 'falling in love'.

Most men and women who love each other and have set up home together want to have children at some time. They will have learned a lot about each other. They will enjoy touching their partner, and feel very much in love when they do. When they are ready to have a child, they have to make sure that a sperm from the man can reach an egg.

Making love

Human eggs are fertilised inside the woman's body. So the man and woman have to make sure that the sperms are put as near as possible to the woman's eggs. They do this by making love.

Just before making love, the man feels excited. His penis becomes erect. It fills with blood.

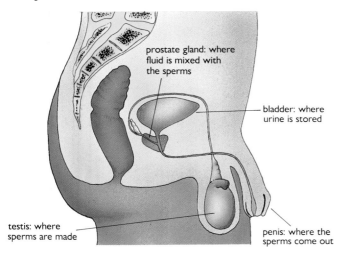

prostate gland: where fluid is mixed with the sperms

bladder: where urine is stored

testis: where sperms are made

penis: where the sperms come out

The woman will also be excited about making love, and will be ready for her partner to push his penis inside her body.

This is very pleasant for both of them, especially when they move the penis in and out. After a while,

the man's muscles automatically force millions of sperms out of the penis and into the woman.

The woman has a supply of eggs in her ovaries. Each month one egg is released. If one sperm reaches the egg at the right time, it may be fertilised. The fertilised egg sticks to the wall of the uterus, which has a very rich blood supply. The egg cell divides rapidly – first into two cells, then into four. Very soon there is a ball of cells called an embryo.

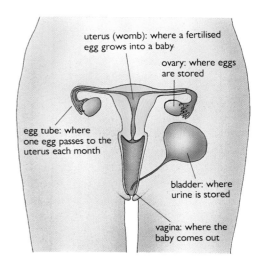

uterus (womb): where a fertilised egg grows into a baby

ovary: where eggs are stored

egg tube: where one egg passes to the uterus each month

bladder: where urine is stored

vagina: where the baby comes out

EXTRAS

1 What would the world be like if we did not need a male and a female to make a new human?

Write a short story about a world where humans reproduce like an amoeba does.

2 Are there any animals that pair for life? What advantage does this have for these animals?

5·9 New humans 2 – eggs and sperms

When a man and a woman make love, it is called sexual intercourse. It is quite natural, just as you eat when you are hungry or sleep when you are tired. The couple enjoy it, and if they did not do it, no babies would be born.

On the other hand, sexual intercourse can produce unwanted children. Also, some diseases can be passed on from one person to another when they make love. AIDS, which reduces resistance to infections, is an example of a disease passed on in this way.

A monthly cycle

Most of the time, sexual intercourse in humans does not lead to an egg being fertilised. The couple may have decided to use a contraceptive to be sure that no sperms reach the egg. Or the woman's body may not have produced an egg at the right time.

When a woman is not pregnant, her body produces an egg each month. And each month, her body prepares itself for a fertilised egg. When a woman becomes pregnant, she stops having periods. This is often the first sign that she may be pregnant.

Preventing unwanted babies

A couple may want to make love, but do not want children. They can do this by avoiding the time in the month when an egg is likely to be fertilised. But it is often hard to know exactly which days to avoid.

The couple may decide to use a contraceptive. A contraceptive like a condom or a cap stops sperms reaching the egg. A contraceptive pill taken by the woman can stop eggs from being released.

Men and women who already have a family may choose to be sterilised. Then the egg or sperm tubes are cut so that the route for the egg or sperm is blocked.

Some men and women do not use contraceptives because of their beliefs.

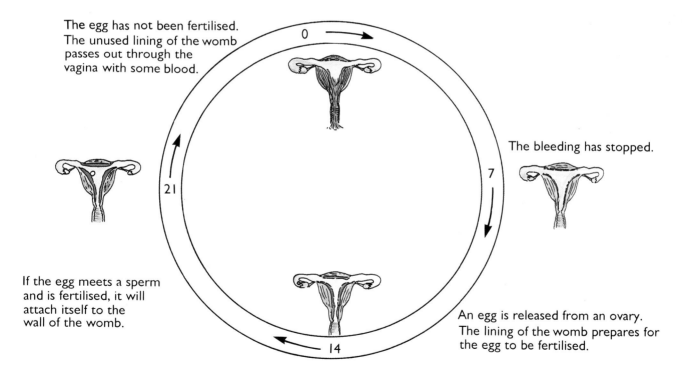

The egg has not been fertilised. The unused lining of the womb passes out through the vagina with some blood.

0

The bleeding has stopped.

7

21

If the egg meets a sperm and is fertilised, it will attach itself to the wall of the womb.

14

An egg is released from an ovary. The lining of the womb prepares for the egg to be fertilised.

EXTRAS

1 Compare the way that humans* reproduce with the way that a different mammal does. Write down all the similarities and differences that you can find.

2 What are the advantages of having a lot of children? What are the disadvantages?

3 Are there any animals, apart from humans, that can choose how many young they have?

5·10 New humans 3 – 'I'm pregnant!'

This short story will give you some idea how much two people who love each other can want a baby.

We had been wanting a baby for ages, and when I missed a period at last, it seemed too good to be true. When it still didn't come after three weeks, I couldn't stand it any longer. On my way to work I took a sample of my urine into the ante-natal clinic at the hospital. The sister was very kind and said I could wait and have the results in about 10 minutes.

I sat there with all sorts of notions going through my mind. Supposing it was negative; how should I react? I mustn't build up my hopes too high; after all, I'd missed periods before, but this time . . .

A nurse came back from the laboratory with a paper in her hand. She grinned at me and then winked as she went into the sister's office. My heart leapt. Sister called me in, and there were the magic words 'pregnancy positive'.

I let out a cry of excitement and hugged the sister. I went through the next ten minutes in a daze, filling in forms and booking appointments. The woman who walked out to the car park was very different from the one who'd gone in 20 minutes earlier. How was I going to keep the news to myself ALL DAY?

I was upstairs, changing out of my working clothes, when I heard her key in the front door.

'Hello, I'm up here.'

'Hello,' she yelled back.

She closed the door and came straightaway up the stairs and into the bedroom. I remember feeling the room suddenly very full, what with the clothes I'd taken off and the ones I was going to put on scattered on the bed. She added to this fullness by walking around me, still with all her winter clothes on.

'Congratulations!' she said all of a sudden. 'I've been to the hospital.'

She grabbed hold of me. I felt a bit silly, standing in my shirt-tails, with my left sock still in my hand.

'You're going to be a daddy!'

All the evening I kept on remembering this and each time I remembered I'd have great waves of happiness and excitement fill me up.

Pregnancy

An embryo develops for about 40 weeks inside its mother before it is born. It gets everything it needs from its mother, and passes all its waste back to her.

Look at the pictures of a human* embryo. Try these questions:

1 How does the embryo get food and oxygen?

2 What protects the embryo?

● Do a line graph that shows how a human* embryo grows in 40 weeks inside its mother.

EXTRAS

1 Why is it better for the embryo to develop inside its mother rather than outside?

2 Twelve-year-old girls are given a rubella injection to stop them from catching German measles. What has this got to do with being pregnant?

3 What should pregnant women avoid doing? Why?

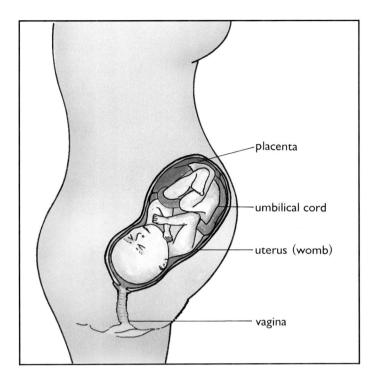

placenta

umbilical cord

uterus (womb)

vagina

Birth

After about 40 weeks, the baby leaves the mother through the vagina. The mother knows the baby is coming because the uterus muscles start to contract. This is called labour – it is hard but exciting work for the mother. She gets help and support from a nurse called a midwife, and from the baby's father.

When the contractions start, the liquid sac that has been protecting the baby bursts. Later, usually after several hours of gradual pushing, the baby is born head first through the vagina. Once the baby's head can be seen from the outside, the rest of the body soon appears.

The parents will want to know if it's a girl or a boy, but the midwife must first make sure the baby is healthy. She cleans it up, and helps it to start breathing if necessary. The umbilical cord that links the baby's blood supply to the mother's is no longer needed. The midwife cuts the cord, then she hands the baby to the mother.

The mother has to wait for the placenta or afterbirth to come away from her uterus. It too is no longer needed. Then the mother can take a well-earned rest.

The baby usually sleeps for a while, but it will soon want some food. Babies have a natural instinct to suck. The mother's body has prepared a natural milky food for the baby in her breasts. As well as being food and drink for the baby, breast milk also helps to protect the baby from diseases.

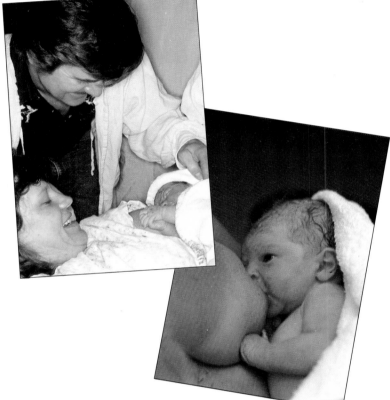

Growing up

● The new baby grows and learns very fast. Can you put these landmarks in the baby's life in order?

– says 'Mum' or 'Dad' – teeth fall out
– crawls – sits up on its own
– walks – goes to school
– stands up – first tooth

EXTRAS

1 What other changes happen to boys and girls between the ages of 10 and 15? Make two lists, one for the girls and one for the boys.

2 Why do these changes happen?

3 Make a list of landmarks in your life. Put birth at one end, and death at the other. Fill in your landmarks so far, then predict what you would like to happen in the future.

● Look at these three families. Your group should choose one of them to discuss. Start with these questions, but you may like to talk about others:
 – Where do you think they are from?
 – How many generations can you see?
 – What do you think each person in the group does during the day?
 – How many children can you see?
 – Why do you think the family has this number of children?

Get each person in your group to choose one of the photos. They should write a short story that describes a day in the life of a child in their photo. Then talk together about what you have written.

Death

Death is just as much a part of life as birth is. But it can be very upsetting, especially if the person is from your own family.

Old people often spend some of their last years talking and playing with their grandchildren. This is one way that they can help others and share their wisdom. They are greatly loved, and will be sadly missed when their bodies finally die. But they leave a great deal behind them. Although you may not realise it, many of your skills and much of your knowledge will have come from your grandparents.

Generations

How much are you like your parents or grandparents? Probably more than you think! You inherit many things from your parents and grandparents. These things are passed on in the egg and sperm that made you. They cannot be changed. An example is the colour of your eyes. But you may be quite different from your parents.

Other things you learn from them, or from other people. An example is your language.

● Try this task – but, be warned, it is tricky! Make three lists: one of features you have inherited, one of things your parents have taught you, and one of things you have learnt from others.

EXTRAS

1 Read about chromosomes* to find out how you inherit features.

2 How are you like your parents? How are you different?

5·13 Populations

The human population of the world is increasing. In 1985 it was estimated at about 4850 million.

Year (A.D.):	1650	1750	1850	1950	2000
World population (millions):	500	700	1000	2500	?

- Plot a line graph of these population figures. Make an estimate from your graph of the world population in 2000.

Living with each other

Some animals are independent. They do not live with other animals of their species. They get all their own food, and look after themselves. They only get together when they have to mate. Other animals, like us, live in large groups.

All animals depend on other organisms in some way or other. Most living things are eaten by others for food. Plants provide oxygen that lets animals breathe. Animals provide carbon dioxide that plants need to make their food.

Use the reference section to help you to answer these questions:

1 Which animals, apart from humans live in large groups?

2 Make three chains of organisms that live off other organisms. One example is: humans live off chickens that live off wheat.

3 Choose three mammals. For each one, say what stops its population from becoming enormous.

EXTRAS: evolution chart

Communicating

An evolution chart tells you which organisms were alive at different times in the past. It also shows how we think organisms have evolved from common origins.

1 (a) Which species is most common now?
(b) Which species have died out?
(c) About how many million years ago did mammals first appear?

2 Which were the most common large animals 100 to 150 million years ago? What has happened to this species since then? Why?

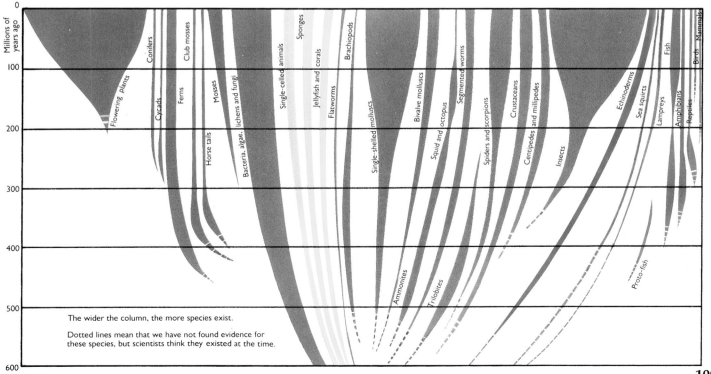

The wider the column, the more species exist.

Dotted lines mean that we have not found evidence for these species, but scientists think they existed at the time.

6 ELECTRICITY

6.1 Switch on!

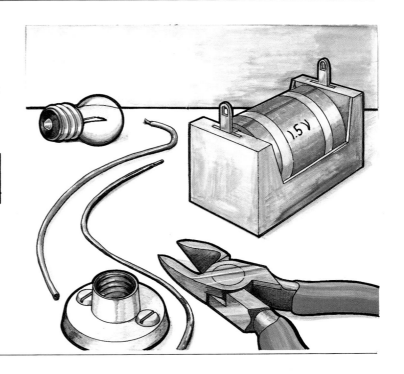

- Can you make this bulb light? To do it, you must make a *circuit*.

1 Why do you think it is called a circuit?

- When you have managed it, do a drawing of what you did. Show all the wires carefully, especially where they join a bulb.
- Write up what you did.

30/4/98   Lighting a bulb

- When the bulb is lit, cut any one of the wires. What happens?
  Never do this with mains wires. ⚠

- Get the bulb to light again. How did you do it?
- Imagine that a friend of yours cannot get his bulb to light. Write him a checklist of things to test to get it working.

Switches

Here are some switches.

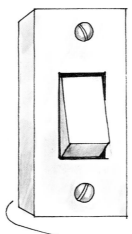
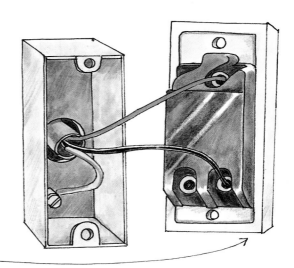

What does a switch do?

- Can you make a switch to turn your bulb on and off? Try it. You will have to work out how to wire it up yourself.

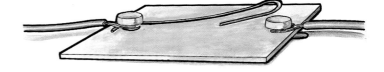

Bulbs

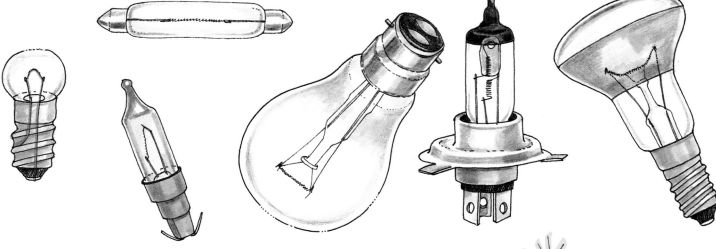

- Do a sketch of each bulb. Draw a red line that shows where the electricity goes when the bulb is alight. The first one has been done for you.

2 What do all these bulbs have that makes them light up?

3 When you made a bulb light up, why did the wire joining the bulb to the battery not light up?

4 What other types of bulb do you know about?

Messing about with bulbs

- Can you:
  - Make two bulbs light, so that when one is unscrewed they both go out?
  - Make two bulbs light, so that when one is unscrewed the other one stays alight?

- Draw your circuits.

- Plan and carry out an experiment to find out if a bulb in the first circuit is as bright as a bulb in the second circuit. Make sure your experiment is fair!

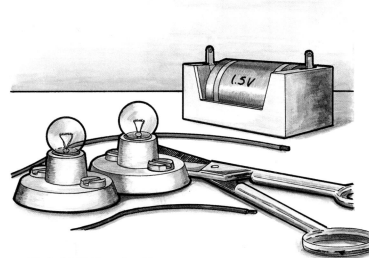

EXTRAS

1 What is the difference between a doorbell switch and a light switch?

Observing

2 Look inside a torch. Work out the path the electricity takes to make the bulb light. Do a drawing of the torch with the electricity's route shown in red. [W]

6·2 Circuits

A tester circuit

Electricity will only flow if a circuit is complete. One break and it stops.

A broken circuit may not seem useful, but it can be used to test other things.

- Make this tester circuit:

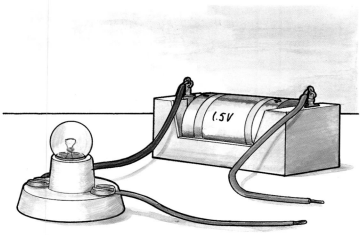

- Find out what happens:
  1 If the two bare wires are touched together.
  2 If the bare wires are touched on the ends of a bare metal wire.
  3 If the bare wires are touched on your skin. (You can try this with wet skin if you want, but remember that you must *never* handle equipment – including wires or switches – with wet hands.)

Things that let electricity through them are called *conductors*.

Things that do *not* let electricity through are called *insulators*.

- Use your tester to make a list of conductors and insulators. Here are two to get you started:

> 4/5/98 Conductors and insulators
>
> These things conduct electricity:
> wire, ...
>
> These things are electrical insulators:
> plastic, ...

- When you have found at least five of each, try to write down the sort of materials that conduct electricity.
- Can you say what sort of things are insulators?

Drawing circuits

Drawing circuits is easier if you use an electrician's symbols. Here is an example:

- Copy the electrician's diagram, and label the battery, the bulb and the wires.

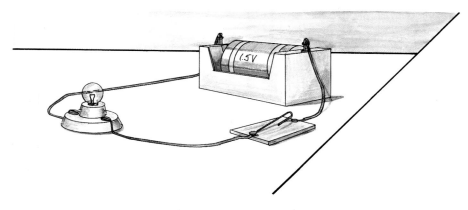

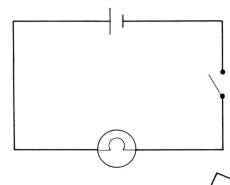

Side-by-side or end-to-end?

This is a *series* circuit. All the bulbs in it are joined end-to-end. There are no branches.
● Make the circuit.
● Find out what happens if all the bulbs are on and you unscrew one of them.
● Get the bulbs working again. Does the same thing happen if you unscrew the others?

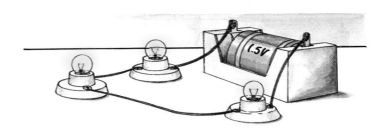

● Draw an electrician's diagram of your circuit.
● Say what happens if you unscrew a bulb. Try to explain what you saw.

This is a *parallel* circuit. It has branches in it. All the bulbs can be put side-by-side.

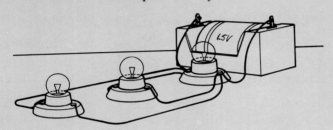

● Make the circuit.
● Do exactly the same tests as you did with the series circuit.
● Draw the circuit diagram and write down everything you see. (Look carefully at the bulbs!)
● Can you explain your results?

● Make a circuit with three bulbs so that one bulb stays on and one bulb goes out when the third is unscrewed.

● Draw the electrician's diagram.
● Is this a series or a parallel circuit? Explain your answer!

A challenge

● Your group can challenge another group. Your group must wire up a circuit with up to three bulbs and one switch in it. You then cover all the wiring up with paper. The other group are allowed to undo the bulbs and press the switch, but they must not look at the wires. They have to work out the wiring. They can do it by making a copy of your circuit, or by drawing the circuit diagram. It is not as easy as it sounds! If they do it, they can make one for you.

1 Draw an electrician's diagram of a circuit where a switch turns a bulb on.

2 What experiments would you do to find out if air is a conductor or an insulator? What might the answer be?

3 Look back at the switches in 6.1. Which parts of the switch are made of insulators? Which parts are made of conductors?

6·3 *Electricity at home 1*

The night the power went off

We always go to Anglesey for our holidays. Our cottage is very quiet, as it is off the beaten track. The last Friday of our holiday last year was Friday the 13th. I remember that it was *too* quiet.

I was watching our portable TV when everything went off. I could only hear our dog Sam's breathing, and I could see nothing. My mum, dad and brother had gone to the pub. After five minutes it was still pitch black, and I was getting worried. I found a candle, but no match. I tried to get the electric fire to light some papers, but the fire had gone off as well. I began to feel cold. There was no way of getting a hot drink without the kettle.

In the end I decided to go to bed. I lay there for a long time thinking about the missing noises: the stereo, the TV, the fridge and the washing machine were all silent. Then I heard a sound. I crept down the stairs. Just as I got to the bottom, Sam barked. I jumped a mile, and banged my head hard on a wooden beam. My brother was there with a torch.

'Everything OK?' he asked, 'There's been a power cut.'

'Really', I replied, 'I'd never have guessed'.

'They couldn't serve beer in the pub because the pumps wouldn't work. And there's been an accident on the main road. A lorry has hit a pole.'

Soon my mum and dad came back. They fixed up some candles. My head was cut, and I held a towel on it. I had to wash it with cold water, and it soon stopped bleeding. Mum tried to throw the towel into the washing machine. When she opened the door, loads of water ran out. It had been halfway through a wash when the power went off. We had forgotten all about it.

When the mess was cleared up, we went to bed. But halfway through the night we all woke up. The dog was barking, the lights were on, the washing machine was going flat out and dad's alarm was buzzing. What a noisy end to a quiet holiday!

Making life easier

● Copy and fill in the table. You can put down any electrical item in your home. You should be able to think of at least twenty. The first one is done for you.

9/5/98	Electricity at home
Item	What the electricity does
TV	Makes sound, makes the screen light up.

- Sort your list in to three or four groups. For example, you could put all the things that produce sound in one group.
- Write the groups, and what they have in common, under your table.

House lights

Here is an electrician's symbol for a switch:

and an electrician's symbol for a light:

- Draw a plan for a bungalow in your book. It does not need to be the same as this one, but make sure you have got all the rooms on.

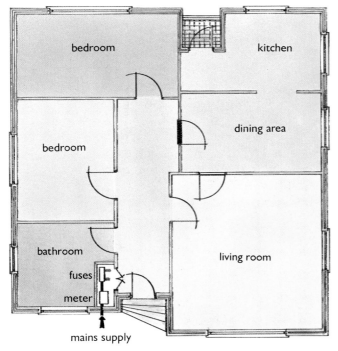

mains supply

- Draw a meter and fuse box in the hall of your bungalow.
- Put light symbols on the plan where you need lights.
- Put switches on the plan where you need switches.
- In a different colour draw in wiring from the fuse box so that the switches will control the lights. Remember that each circuit must start from the brown wire at the fuse box, and finish at the blue wire at the fuse box.

- You may be able to make and wire up a model of a house yourself.

A staircase light
You will need:
- two two-way paper fastener switches
- one bulb
- five bits of connecting wire
- one battery

- Your job is to find a way of wiring up the switches so that they are like the switches at the two ends of a staircase.

    If the light is ON, switching either switch will turn it OFF.

    If the light is OFF, switching either switch will turn it ON.

    Make sure that your switches are always connected to one of their two contacts.

- Draw an electrician's diagram of your circuit.

EXTRAS

1 Think of three reasons why power cuts could be dangerous.

2 Look through the list you made of electrical items in your house. How many use batteries? Are any of these used to produce heat? Can you explain this?

6·4 Magnets

You can use electricity to make a magnet.
- Your job is to make the strongest magnet you can. Use a battery, wire and nail.

  Before you start, decide how will you measure the strength of the magnet. You have a compass and some paper clips to help you.

Warning: Only join your magnet to the battery for a short time. If you do it for more than a few seconds, the battery will quickly go flat.

- Have a competition with another group. See who can make the strongest magnet. Remember, if you leave your battery connected, it will go flat. You must agree a fair measuring system with the other group.
- When you have finished, do a report on your work. You should say:
  - what you did to make a magnet.
  - how you tested it.
  - how you made it strong.
  - how you compared the strength of two magnets.

Testing magnets

Electromagnets are used for picking up metal at a scrap yard.

Investigating

- Answer as many of these questions about electromagnets as you can. You will have to do experiments for most of them.

1 What sort of material makes a good core for an electromagnet?

2 Does it matter which way the wire is coiled round the core?

3 Do more turns of wire make the magnet stronger?

4 Which part of the coil is the most magnetic?

5 What sort of materials will your electromagnet pick up?

Electric buzzers

Making a buzzer

● Make a buzzer like this:

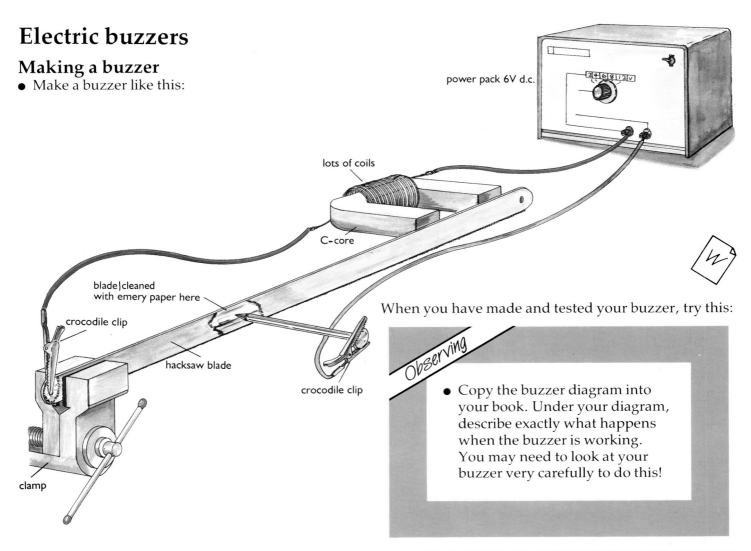

power pack 6V d.c.

lots of coils

C-core

blade|cleaned with emery paper here

crocodile clip

hacksaw blade

crocodile clip

clamp

When you have made and tested your buzzer, try this:

Observing

● Copy the buzzer diagram into your book. Under your diagram, describe exactly what happens when the buzzer is working. You may need to look at your buzzer very carefully to do this!

Permanent magnets

Some pieces of metal are magnets without needing electricity. They are called permanent magnets.

● Use a permanent magnet to find out:
  – where the poles are (these are the places which pins or nails stick to best).
  – what happens when you float one in a Petri dish (try to turn the dish round!).
  – which other materials will stick to it, and which will not.
  – what happens when you take it near the poles of another magnet.

EXTRAS

1 Why do scrap yards use electromagnets instead of ordinary cranes?

2 Which parts of a car would the electromagnet *not* be able to pick up?

3 Which items in your home have magnets in? Can you think of a good way of finding out?

4 Investigate permanent magnets. Find out how the force between the poles of two magnets depends on the distance the two magnets are apart. You will have to use strong magnets, and to measure very small (1–5mm) distances. Use a newton meter to measure the force.

6·5 Getting hot

Electricity is often used to make heat.

Many things that use electricity get hot although they are not supposed to.

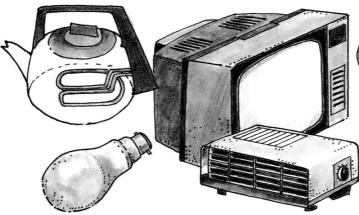
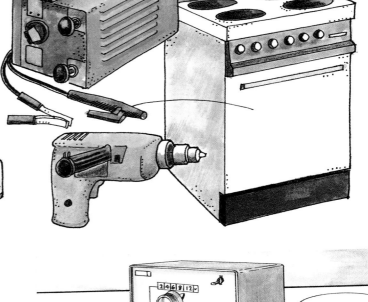

- Write down two groups of things that use electricity. Put those that are meant to get hot in one list. Put the things that get hot but are not meant to in the other.

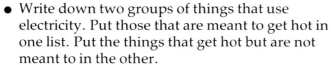

- Use the equipment to find out if a car headlamp bulb produces heat. Think what you will do before you start.
- Write up your findings when you have finished.
- Try the experiment with different-sized bulbs. Ask your teacher to check your circuit *before* you switch on. Does the size of the bulb affect how much heat it gives off? Is there any information on the bulb that might explain your results?

Hot wires

- Make this circuit:

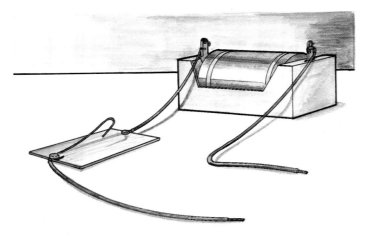

- Make sure the switch if OFF (not connected). Fit a piece of very thin wire across the gap. A single strand of steel wool will do.
- Watch very carefully. Do not touch the wire. Turn the switch ON so that electricity flows in the thin wire.
  - What do you see?
  - What happens to the wire?
  - Can you explain it?
- If you can, try some other thin wires.

Take great care to turn the switch OFF before you put a new wire in the circuit. You may burn yourself if you leave the switch on. If the wire does not burn, touch a small piece of paper on it to see if it is hot. **Do not touch it with your fingers.**

Fuses

A mistake in the wiring and this is what can happen! The electricity has produced too much heat and caused a fire.

This can usually be prevented by using a fuse. Every mains plug has a fuse in it, and most electrical things have fuses inside them as well. A fuse is a thin wire. Its job is to break when too much electricity flows in a circuit. It stops the wires in the circuit from melting and so prevents expensive items from being damaged.

When the mixer is turned on, electricity flows from the mains and through the fuse. The fuse wire is chosen so that it does not get hot when the motor is working properly.

Sometimes, too much electricity can go into the mixer. This may happen because the wiring inside has been damaged or because the motor is being overworked. The extra electricity makes the fuse wire get hot and melt. When the wire melts, the fuse has 'blown'. Electricity cannot flow through a blown fuse, so there is no risk of a fire in the mixer.

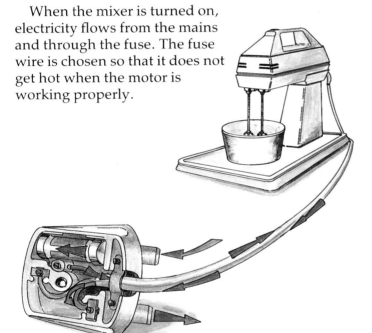

Ratings

Look at the fuses above. They all have a number on them, like 13A or 30A. This is the rating of the fuse. The A stands for amps. Amps are a measure of how much electricity the fuse can let through without blowing.

- Look at the rating and the thickness of each fuse. What sort of rating do thin fuses have? What about thick ones?

EXTRAS

1 There is probably only one fuse for all your house lights. Why? Where is the fuse?

2 Most fuse wires are put in 'cartridges'. The cartridges are made from china. Why are the wires in cartridges? Why are these made from china?

3 The Electricity Council recommends that appliances up to 720 watts should be fitted with 3 amp fuses. Appliances over 720 watts should have 13 amp fuses. The watt rating is a measure of how much electricity an object uses each second. This rating is normally marked on the object.

What fuse would you use for these objects?
(a) a table lamp
(b) a radio
(c) a TV
(d) a washing machine
(e) a microwave oven

⚠ You may need to look at the back of some of these things to check their watt rating. Be careful – first make sure each object is switched off and unplugged from the mains.

6·6 Batteries

1 Why are there so many different sorts of battery?

2 Do big batteries light bulbs better than small ones?

3 Are high-voltage batteries better or worse (or more dangerous!) than low-voltage ones?

Is big better?

- Design an experiment to find out what difference the size of a battery makes to the way it lights a bulb. Use three or four different types of battery that are all marked 1.5V.
- Get your teacher's approval, then carry out your experiment and write up your results. What difference does size make?

- How else can you find out what difference size makes? Design at least one other experiment to find out how large batteries are different from small ones. Try it out if you can.

Are volts valuable?

- Find out how a high-voltage battery is different from a low-voltage one. Take great care only to use a bulb which has a voltage rating near the rating of the high voltage battery. If you do not, you will waste a lot of bulbs.
- Write your results up carefully.

4 The car battery and the nickel–cadmium battery are rechargeable.
   (a) What does this mean?
   (b) How are they recharged?
   (c) How would you decide if it was worth the extra money to buy a rechargeable battery instead of an ordinary one?

5 Is a watch battery cheap or expensive at about £2? Explain your answer.

Planning

- Plan an experiment to find out if it is better value to buy a long-life battery or a normal one.

120

What are volts?

The voltage is how much of a kick the electricity is given as it leaves the battery. The kick always gets used up in the circuit joined to the battery. So electricity with a big kick can light up a lot of bulbs. Electricity with a small kick can only light a few.

- Connect up each of the circuits shown below. Take care to use the right bulb.

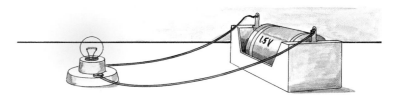

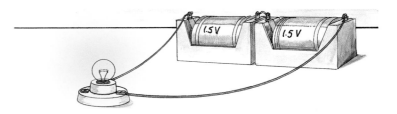

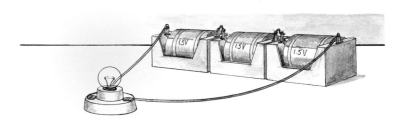

6 What difference do more batteries make to the bulb?

- Write a summary of your experiment. Explain what you saw.
- Find out and explain what happens if you have one of the batteries connected the 'wrong' way round.

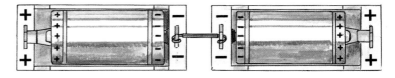

- What will happen if you turn two round? Try it.

EXTRAS

1 What sort of battery would you need for an electric car to go on the road?

2 A 9V battery is made from small 1.5V batteries. Do a design that shows what the 9V battery might be like inside.

3 (a) Find out the prices of different 1.5V batteries. How does the size of a battery affect its cost?

(b) Look at the prices of batteries that have different voltages. How does a battery's voltage affect its cost?

6·7 Electricity at home 2

What are the mains?

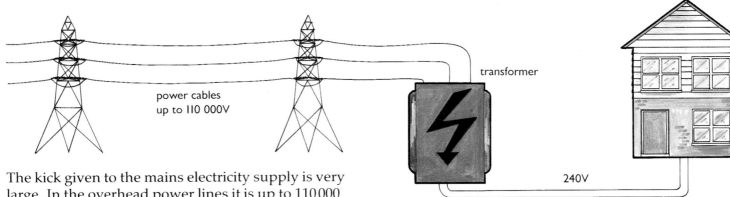

power cables
up to 110 000V

transformer

240V

The kick given to the mains electricity supply is very large. In the overhead power lines it is up to 110000 volts. This is cut down to 240 volts before it gets to your house, but that is still a big kick. So the electricity can do lots of jobs in your house.

● How many batteries would you need to get a 240V kick?

Even if you did connect up all these batteries, they would still not be the same as the mains. Batteries give a steady voltage. The mains voltage changes all the time; it is called an alternating current. For some uses, like heating and lights, this does not matter. But for others, like radios or computers, you need a steady voltage. In a computer, there is a transformer to change the mains voltage from 240V to 12V or 5V, and a rectifier to change it from an alternating to a steady current.

240V mains supply

output chips

network interface

input chips, central processor and disc interface

transformer and rectifier

RAM (random access memory) and ROM (read only memory) chips

Safety first

All house wiring has a safety circuit called an earth circuit. The large pin on the plugs in your house is for an earth wire.

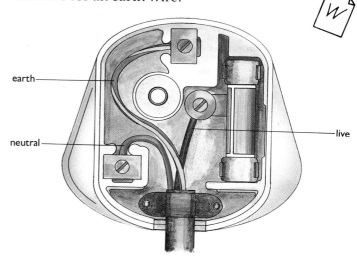

earth
neutral
live

Another problem with mains electricity is that it is dangerous. At 240 volts the electricity has enough of a kick to give your body a big kick, and even to kill you. So it has to be used carefully.

Why have an earth wire?

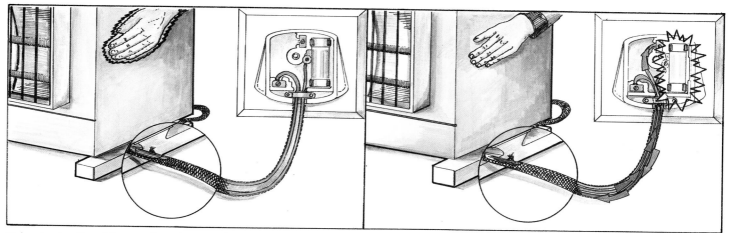

No earth wire. Electricity goes through you to the ground. You could be killed.

As soon as the bare wire touches the metal, electricity flows to the ground through the earth wire. This blows the fuse. Then there is no danger.

- Use two diagrams to explain how an earth wire makes the fire safer.

Some electrical items do not have earth wires. They have plastic cases which cannot become live.

EXTRAS

1 Do a safety check on electrical things at school or at home.

 Take care – do not undo plugs without an adult's help.

Make a list of all the items you check. Note any faults. Say how you would make them safe. Do a labelled drawing of a properly wired plug. Colour in the parts of the plug that conduct electricity.

2 Modern houses and laboratories do not have fuses. They have special trip switches instead. All the house or lab wires go through the trip switch box. If any electricity flows in the earth wire, the trip switch operates and stops the electricity flowing down the live wire.

Do a design to show how a trip switch might work. Show clearly which wire is which, and explain how you think it would work. You will probably need to use an electromagnet in your design. Real trip switches contain some complicated electronics, so do not expect to make one!

Shocks and flashes

There are some very big voltages around us all the time.

These big voltages are made when electricity builds up in one place. The flash or the shock happens when the electricity flows somewhere else very quickly, usually into the ground. The shock is very dangerous if there is a lot of electricity and if it flows through a person on its way to the ground.

How do water and warmth affect electricity?

You need to use some objects you tested earlier on which electricity builds up.

- Build up electricity on each one by rubbing it with a cloth. Then find out what these things do to the electricity:
  – Making the object damp (not dripping wet!)
  – Making the object warm (not hot). You can do this by holding it a long way above a safe Bunsen flame.
  – Touching the 'electrified' part of the object with your fingers before testing it.

Making electricity – a Van de Graaff generator

1 Where does the electricity come from?
2 Where does the electricity build up?
3 Why does the machine have a belt in it?
4 Why is the belt made of rubber?
5 What voltage builds up on the dome?
6 Why doesn't this kill the girl holding the dome?
7 Why do you think the girl's hair stands on end?
8 Why won't the machine work well on a rainy day?

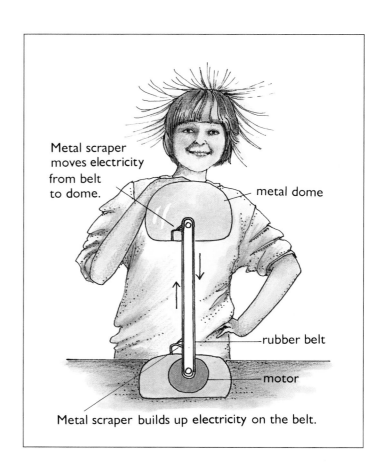

Metal scraper moves electricity from belt to dome.

metal dome

rubber belt

motor

Metal scraper builds up electricity on the belt.

Making electricity – lightning

On a hot day, the land is baked by the sun. The air over the land gets hot and rises. Cold air flows down to take the place of the hot air. The hot air rubs on the cold air, building up large amounts of electricity.

The electricity charges build up to several million volts. The electricity then flows to the ground incredibly fast and makes a spark and a bang. Because a lot of electricity flows in these sparks, they are very dangerous.

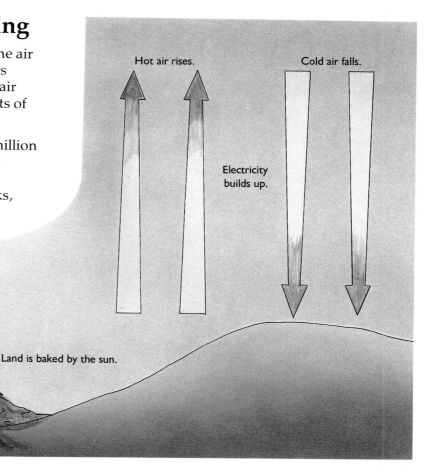

Hot air rises.

Cold air falls.

Electricity builds up.

Land is baked by the sun.

Communicating

- Find out as much as you can about thunder and lightning. Use the library or any other books you have. Now imagine you are talking to a friend who doesn't understand how lightning happens. Explain what makes the flashes and the bangs.

EXTRAS

1 You are caught in an electrical storm in the mountains. All the metal items you are carrying are buzzing (rather like a power line does on a damp day). Where should you shelter? Why? Where should you *not* shelter?

2 Tall buildings like churches have lightning conductors. Find out what they are made of and how they work.

3 You can build up a big charge on your body if you walk on a nylon carpet. Then you get a painful shock if you touch a metal object like a radiator.
(**a**) Why does the electricity build up?
(**b**) Explain why you get a shock.
(**c**) Think of some ways of avoiding getting shocks like this.

6·9 Electrical signals 1

As well as being used for power, heat and light, electricity can be used to send signals or messages.

A burglar alarm

A burglar alarm uses an electrical signal. The burglar is detected by a *sensor*. The sensor sends a signal that operates an *output*.

A switch is one type of sensor. A bulb is one type of output.

- Design and make a simple burglar alarm that will light a bulb when a door or window is opened. You could use kitchen foil to make a 'moving' switch.
- When you have made and tested your alarm, find out a way of wiring it up to two or three different windows. Opening any one of them should light the bulb.
- Write up your work. Draw a diagram of your circuit.

1 Your alarm is obviously not like a real one. How would you need to change it if you were actually going to put it in a house?

An air traffic control room. Electricity is used to send signals by telephone, radio and television. Can you think of any other examples from your own life?

Intruder alarms

Your simple alarm only had a sensor and an output. Professional alarms have a control box between the sensor and the output. The control box can do all sorts of things. For example:

- If you open the door, it gives you 30 seconds before ringing the alarm. This gives you time to turn if off with a key if it is your house.
- When the alarm is turned on, the control box *latches* it. This means that even if you shut the door or window, the alarm will keep ringing.

2 What other things do you think the control box should do?

Where there's smoke there's fire

There can be many people in a big school, office or department store. A fire in one of these places can be very serious and claim many lives. One way of protecting the people in a large building is to fit smoke sensors. These give early warning of a fire. The fire service then have time to get people out of the building and put the fire out.

Usually smoke sensors are fitted in all the main areas of the building. They are connected in the same circuit so that any one can start the alarm ringing.

The most common smoke sensors use a light beam to detect smoke. If the smoke is likely to be grey or white then the sensor detects light reflected by the smoke.

If the smoke is black, as it could be in some factories, then the smoke breaks a light beam to the sensor.

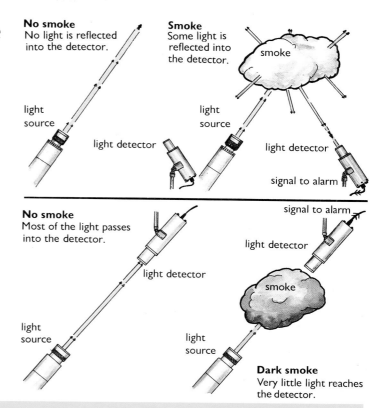

No smoke
No light is reflected into the detector.

light source

light detector

Smoke
Some light is reflected into the detector.

smoke

light source

light detector

signal to alarm

No smoke
Most of the light passes into the detector.

light detector

light source

signal to alarm

light detector

smoke

light source

Dark smoke
Very little light reaches the detector.

Communicating

3 Why are smoke sensors all connected into the same circuit?

4 Why are there two types of smoke sensor?

5 Which type of sensor would you put in your home? Why?

6 In a building where there are many smoke sensors, would they be connected in series or parallel to an alarm? Explain your choice.

● Draw a diagram to show how the sensor is arranged to detect *black* smoke.

A fire alarm

7 What sort of sensor would you need to make a fire alarm? Would it be:
   – something that melts at a low temperature?
   – something that changes when it is hot?
   – something that bends when it is hot?
   – something that can detect smoke?

8 What sort of output will you need?

● Design a fire alarm. Do a careful drawing with labels. Your teacher will be able to give you some help about the sort of sensor to use.

● Check with your teacher before you make and test your fire alarm.

● Write up what happens.

● Make a list of all the faults in your alarm. Suggest some ways that you could get round them with more expensive equipment.

EXTRAS

1 The heat in your home is probably controlled by electrical signals. Find out:
(a) what sort of sensor is used.
(b) what happens when the room is hot.
(c) what happens when the room is cold.

2 Look back at the washing machine programme in 2.7.
(a) What sensors would there be in the washing machine?
(b) What outputs are there?

Brain death

Sometimes it is not easy to tell if a person is dead. They may stop breathing for a while, their heart may stop, but there is still a chance they may live if the brain shows some activity.

When a person has died, doctors first check some of the muscles' reactions. They see if the patient reacts to touch or pain. They shine a bright light into the eye to check if the eye muscles react to it. Doctors do this test because muscles are connected to the brain by nerves.

Your brain controls most of your body movements by sending messages to the muscles. These messages are tiny electrical impulses that travel along the nerve fibres. So when your body's sensors pick up information such as heat, light or touch, they send it to your brain (the control centre). The brain tells your muscles how to react, and their movements are the output.

The body's electrical impulses can be picked up by sensors in special machines, and displayed on paper or a screen. If a machine shows no electrical impulses in the brain, a person is said to be brain dead.

A portable EEG (electroencephalograph). This machine records the electrical signals from the brain and converts them into traces on paper

Testing your nerves

Try to find out where there are most sensors in your partner's skin. You will need:
– a sheet of paper to record your results
– a piece of wire
– a blindfold

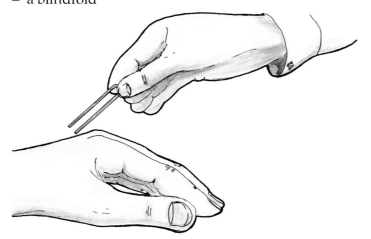

- Before starting, decide:
  – how many tests you need in each place
  – how you will record the results
  – how you can use others in your group to check your results

- Blindfold one person in your group.
- Bend the wire over so that you have two points about 5mm apart and next to each other.
- Press the end of the wire gently on your partner's bare arm. You can use one point or both points. Ask your partner how many points she or he can feel.
- Repeat the test as many times as you think you need.
- Then try part of their hand, and finally their fingers.
- Write up your results. Explain carefully what you did to make sure that the experiment was fair.

Electric defence

Some animals use electricity to keep other animals away, and to kill their food.

The electric eel is one of the most feared of South American fish. It stings up to six times in less than 1/200th of a second. Each sting carries a shock of about 500 volts – enough to kill a man.

The stingray uses electricity to defend itself. A fish that attacks a stingray is likely to get a shock of 200 volts. The ray also uses shocks to stun its own food before eating it.

Reaction speed

How fast do you think the electrical signals in your body travel? You can make an estimate in an experiment like the one below.

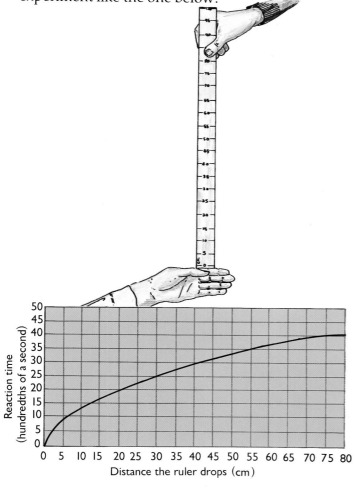

Reaction time (hundredths of a second) vs *Distance the ruler drops (cm)*

- Get your partner to hold a metre rule so that it is vertical, with the 0 mark at the bottom. Put the palm of your hand, fingers and thumb straight, across the ruler so that the top of your hand is level with the 0 line. The ruler should *not* touch your palm.
- Look at the ruler, but not at your partner. When she drops it, catch it as quickly as you can.
- Repeat the experiment several times, and work out the average distance that the ruler fell. Use the graph on the left to convert the distance into a falling time.
- Make an estimate of the distance that the electrical signals had to travel in your partner's body. Remember to measure from *sensor* to *control device* to *output*.
- Use a calculator to work out the speed: divide the distance the signal travelled by the time it took (the ruler's falling time). If you measured in centimetres, divide by 100 to convert to metres per second. 20 metres per second is about 60 miles per hour.

Two extra tests

- Collect all the reaction times for your class. Think of a good way of displaying them. Do the girls have quicker reaction times than the boys?
- Repeat the experiment above, but with your eyes shut. Make sure that the ruler just touches your palm before it is dropped. How does this affect the results? Can you explain why?

EXTRAS

1 A car driver must have good reactions.

(**a**) What sensors does a driver use?
(**b**) What control device does he or she use?
(**c**) What outputs does he or she use?
(**d**) Make a list of things that could slow down a driver's reactions.

2 Make a list of all the sensors that your body has. Beside each sensor write down: where the sensor is, what could make it send a signal to the brain, and what the output is (or might be).

Controlling a railway

Electrical signals are used to control the railways. They can tell if a train passes, switch a point, and signal the train driver to stop.

Railway lights use a system called 'dual aspect signalling'. Look at these lights:

1 Can you explain why railways use such a complicated system? Wouldn't red and green on their own be enough?

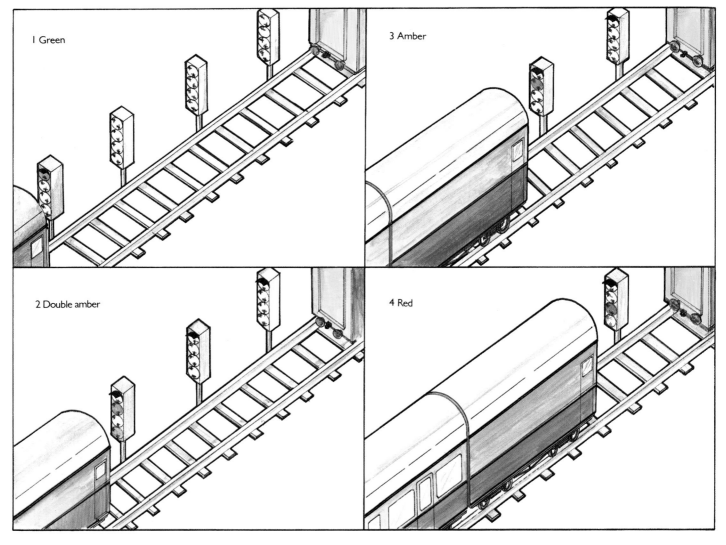

1 Green

3 Amber

2 Double amber

4 Red

Making a model signal

You will need four bulbs. You could colour them (one red, two amber and one green) with felt-tipped pens to make the model more realistic.

- Use two pieces of copper wire to represent each section of track; you need to have four sections of track altogether.
- Put your four bulbs at the start of the first section.
- Join the copper wires with Sellotape – do not let one piece of copper wire touch the next.
- Use a metal object as the train. Lay it across the wires in the first section. Which bulb should it light up?
- Find a way of wiring this section of track to a battery and the right bulb.

- When you have this working, move the 'train' down each section in turn. Get it to light the right bulbs each time.
- When you have finished, ask another group to check that your work is right.
- Draw a diagram of your circuits.

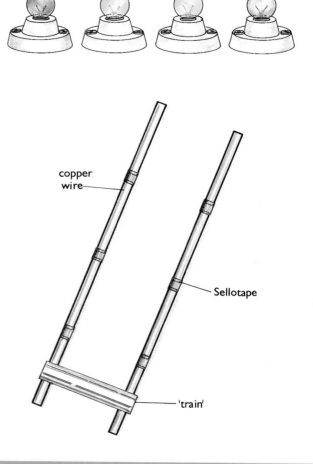

copper wire

Sellotape

'train'

2 What could go wrong with your system?
3 Why could it be dangerous?
4 What could you do to make it more reliable?

Real-life railway sensors do not pass a signal through the train. They use a device called an inductor. This sends a signal if a large metal object moves across it.

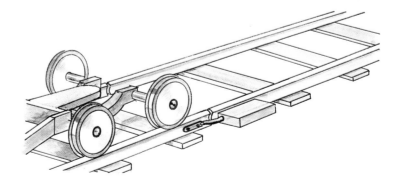

5 Why is this better than the method you used to detect your train?

EXTRAS

1 Does a train really need a driver? Do a design of a section of railway, including a station, which is completely automatic. Show all the sensors you would use, the control boxes you would need, and what they would control.

2 Do a design of a road junction controlled by traffic lights. Mark on it the lights and the sensors you would need. Write a set of instructions for the control box at the junction. They could start 'The main road light is red, the side road is green. When a car comes up the main road then turn the side road light amber.'

6:12 _Investigating home-made batteries_

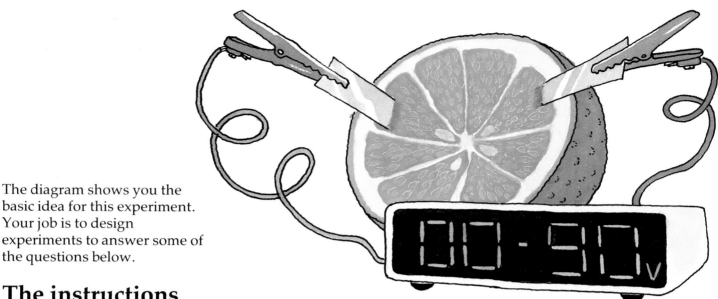

The diagram shows you the basic idea for this experiment. Your job is to design experiments to answer some of the questions below.

The instructions

- Decide which question you want to try.
- Plan what you are going to do: decide what you will need to alter and what you will keep the same.
- Put a date and a title for your experiment in your book.

- Write a few sentences to explain your plan.
- Get your teacher's permission, then do your experiment. Write your results down as you do it.
- Write down what the experiment told you about the question you worked out.
- Either try another question or tidy up.

Investigating

The questions   Try only one at a time!

1 Do different fruits give different voltages?

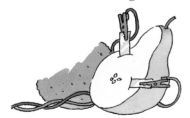

2 Do different metals give different voltages?

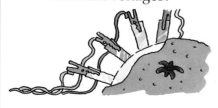

3 How does the distance between the metals affect the voltage?

4 How does the size of the piece of metal affect the voltage?

5 Which fruit and metals give the biggest voltage?

6 Can you find a fruit and two metals that will light a light-emitting diode?

7 Can you get a bigger voltage by joining more metals and fruits?

The first batteries

The first battery was made of pieces of silver and zinc. The metals were separated by bits of card. The whole battery had to be soaked in salt water to make it work.

You can make a battery like this, but you will probably have to use copper instead of silver!

- Find out:
  - why Volta used lots of pieces of metal instead of just one or two.
  - why the battery had to be soaked in salt water.

Allessandro Volta demonstrating his battery to Napoleon

Testing a rechargeable battery

You will need:
- 2 pieces of lead
- 2 wires and crocodile clips
- power supply set at 4 volts
- a torch bulb in a holder
- half a beaker of diluted sulphuric acid – **care!**

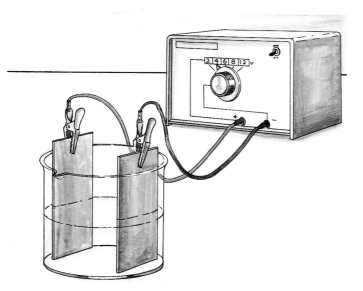

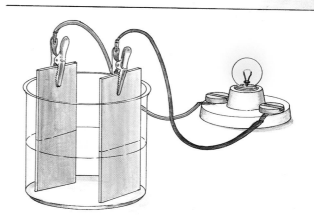

- Switch the power on. Watch the plates carefully. What do you see?
  Leave the power on for a few minutes.

- Turn the power off. Connect the plates to the bulb. What happens?

- Find out if you can re-charge the plates.

- Try this investigation: Does the bulb stay alight longer if the plates are charged for longer? Think carefully how you can do this, then try it out.

- Write up your investigation carefully. Can you do a graph of your results?

5 LIFE

Reference section

Classification

This is not a complete classification tree. Each of the "branches" can be divided up even further.

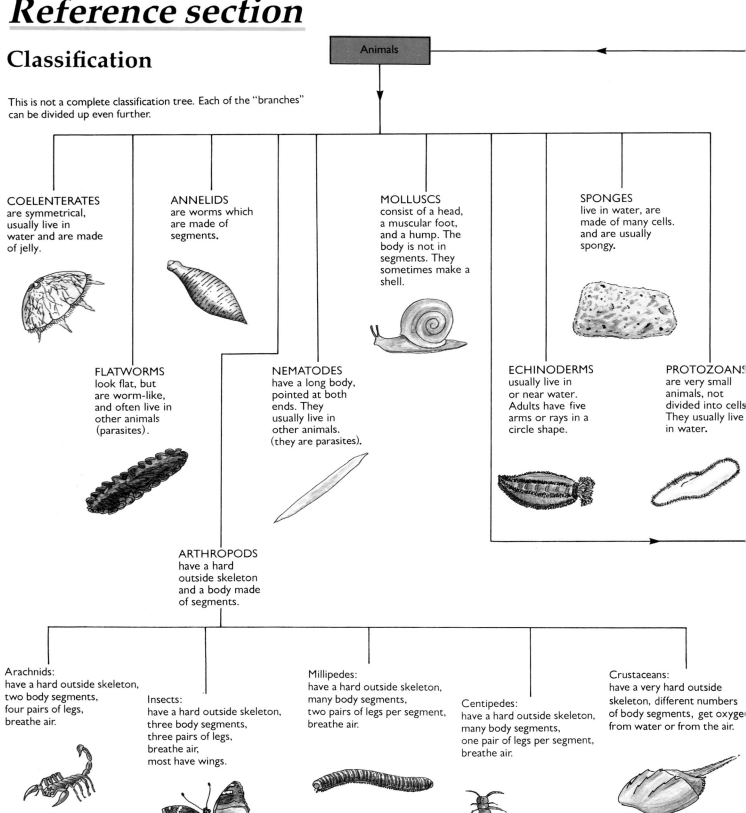

Animals

COELENTERATES are symmetrical, usually live in water and are made of jelly.

ANNELIDS are worms which are made of segments.

MOLLUSCS consist of a head, a muscular foot, and a hump. The body is not in segments. They sometimes make a shell.

SPONGES live in water, are made of many cells. and are usually spongy.

FLATWORMS look flat, but are worm-like, and often live in other animals (parasites).

NEMATODES have a long body, pointed at both ends. They usually live in other animals. (they are parasites).

ECHINODERMS usually live in or near water. Adults have five arms or rays in a circle shape.

PROTOZOANS are very small animals, not divided into cells. They usually live in water.

ARTHROPODS have a hard outside skeleton and a body made of segments.

Arachnids: have a hard outside skeleton, two body segments, four pairs of legs, breathe air.

Insects: have a hard outside skeleton, three body segments, three pairs of legs, breathe air, most have wings.

Millipedes: have a hard outside skeleton, many body segments, two pairs of legs per segment, breathe air.

Centipedes: have a hard outside skeleton, many body segments, one pair of legs per segment, breathe air.

Crustaceans: have a very hard outside skeleton, different numbers of body segments, get oxygen from water or from the air.

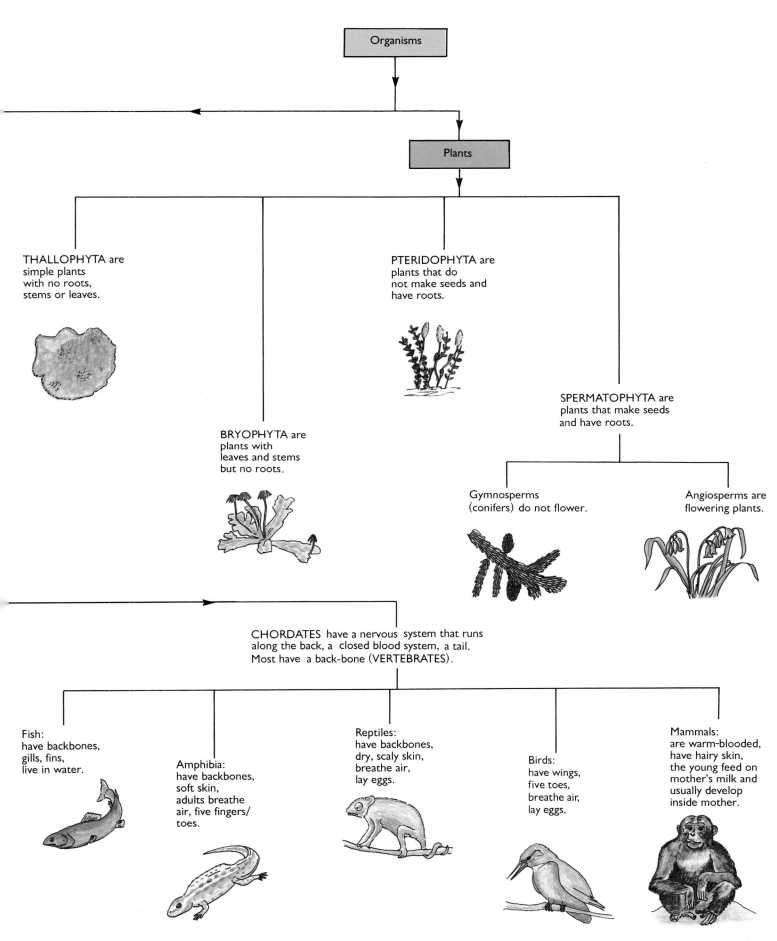

Organisms

Plants

THALLOPHYTA are simple plants with no roots, stems or leaves.

BRYOPHYTA are plants with leaves and stems but no roots.

PTERIDOPHYTA are plants that do not make seeds and have roots.

SPERMATOPHYTA are plants that make seeds and have roots.

Gymnosperms (conifers) do not flower.

Angiosperms are flowering plants.

CHORDATES have a nervous system that runs along the back, a closed blood system, a tail. Most have a back-bone (VERTEBRATES).

Fish: have backbones, gills, fins, live in water.

Amphibia: have backbones, soft skin, adults breathe air, five fingers/toes.

Reptiles: have backbones, dry, scaly skin, breathe air, lay eggs.

Birds: have wings, five toes, breathe air, lay eggs.

Mammals: are warm-blooded, have hairy skin, the young feed on mother's milk and usually develop inside mother.

An alphabetical guide to some organisms

These pages contain information on a variety of living things and how they reproduce.

Algae

Most algae are water plants. They are usually green, but can be red or brown. They have no roots, stems or leaves, but some of them can move.

The smallest and simplest algae are single cells like the *Euglena*.

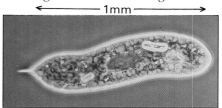
← 1mm →

More complicated seaweed algae can be up to 100 metres long.

Algae get their energy from the sun. They use it to make food like other plants. They reproduce by splitting, but they can also make sex cells. The male cells from one plant join with the female cells from another plant to make spores, which grow into new plants. Algae are important for us: they provide food for animals, and one type of alga purifies sewage.

Amoebae

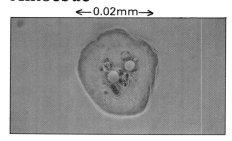
← 0.02mm →

An amoeba is a tiny water animal made of only one cell. It moves along the bottom of ponds by changing shape and spreading, rather like a runny jelly. Bacteria and small plants are its main food. It eats by surrounding its food with part of its body, and then digesting it with chemicals.

Amoebae reproduce by simple cell division. Males and females look exactly the same, and do not need to mate to make new amoebae. The new amoeba is exactly like its parent. If you think about it, an amoeba lives for ever – if nothing eats it!

Aphids

Aphids are tiny insects that live on plant sap. They have small soft bodies, sometimes coloured to match the plant they feed on. They are very common in gardens in summer; you can often see them on rosebuds. Some aphids can fly, but most have no wings.

Aphids have a strange way of reproducing. There are male and female aphids, but the female can have baby aphids without her eggs being fertilised. This means that a female can land on a plant and give birth to lots of young aphids. As the young can reproduce themselves after only a few days, the aphid population soon grows. Aphids are a pest in the garden, and gardeners often spray them with poison to kill them.

Bacteria

Bacteria are tiny cells. They are found everywhere, from the inside of your body to the bottom of the sea. Some bacteria live on other organisms, for example on dying plants. Others can use the sun's energy to make food like plants do.

Bacteria cause many diseases. Typhoid and tetanus are both caused by poisons from bacteria. Other bacteria are helpful: they

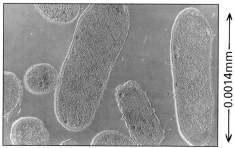
0.0014mm

are used to make yoghurt, cheese and some antibiotics.

To reproduce, bacteria use simple cell division. One cell simply divides into two cells. This can happen very fast: in good conditions a cell can divide once an hour. This means that bacteria spread rapidly. You have probably suffered from this: sickness and diarrhoea are often caused by bacteria. The illness comes on quickly because the bacteria reproduce so fast.

Bracken

Bracken is a fern plant. Like most plants it makes its own food using energy from the sun. Ferns have roots underground so that they can get water and minerals. They have green fronds or leaves that use the sun's energy to make food.

Bracken does not have flowers. It makes spores to reproduce. Spores are like seeds, but they are usually smaller because they do not have a food store with them.

In the summer, bracken makes spores in capsules under the fronds. When conditions are dry, the capsules spring open, throwing the spores into the air. When a spore germinates, it develops male and female parts. In wet weather, the male cells swim to the female cells and fertilise them. The fertilised cells grow into new bracken plants.

Chickens

Although chicken eggs are used by humans for food, most eggs that you buy are not fertile. The hen they come from has usually not mated with a cock, so no sperms have reached the eggs. To produce a baby chick, a cock and a hen must mate.

Chickens and most other birds do not have the same reproductive organs as humans. Both the cock and the hen have an opening called a cloaca near their tails. When they mate, the cock jumps on the hen bird, and the two cloacas are joined. Sperms pass from the cock to the hen through the cloaca. The sperms fertilise the hen's eggs, which develop in her uterus. Just before the egg is laid, an eggshell forms around it. The shell's job is to stop the egg from drying out after it is laid. It is shaped to stop the egg from rolling away.

The eggs are laid in a nest, which insulates them. They are kept warm by the female who sits on them to incubate the embryo chicks. The eggs hatch about three weeks after incubation.

Cod

If you eat fish and chips, you probably eat cod. It is a large fish, often over a metre long, which is found in the sea around Britain. It prefers to live near the sea-bed, so it is caught by a method called trawling: by a net dragged along the bottom of the sea.

Like all fish, there are male and female cod. In the spring, the female fish lays thousands of eggs. A male who has been attracted by the female squirts his sperm over the eggs. Many eggs do not get fertilised, but some do. The eggs are an important food for many fish, including other cod! So there have to be a lot of eggs if any are to survive. The

eggs that survive hatch out as young cod. They are very small, and are also food for other fish.

Earthworms

There are probably over a hundred worms in a square metre of grass meadow. They are very useful because their burrowing mixes up the soil and helps to keep it fertile. As they burrow, they eat rotting leaves and other organic material in the soil: this is their food.

All earthworms are made of segments. They have no backbone, but every worm has both male and female parts. To mate, two worms lie head to tail.

Each worm passes sperms to the other worm. They separate, and each worm mixes the sperms with its own eggs in a moist band. The band is left in the soil where it becomes a cocoon with about 20 eggs in. The eggs hatch several months later. Worms that survive the first few days of life can live up to ten years. Take care next time you dig a piece of ground!

Elephants

Elephants are the largest land mammals. They are plant-eaters and eat huge quantities of food. A full-grown male needs about 90kg of plant food each day. Female elephants live in herds which contain several families, but no adult males. The males live on their own, near but not with the herd. When a female is ready to mate, she leaves the herd to mate, and then returns. After mating, an egg is fertilised inside the

female's body, and develops as an embryo for nearly two years. When the calf is born, it weighs about 100kg, as much as a very large man. The calf feeds on its mother's milk for up to five years, and the rest of the herd protect it. It will take another 21 years before it is fully grown.

Firs

Fir trees keep their leaves all the year round. They are sometimes called evergreens because of this. Firs can stand colder and windier conditions than trees that lose their leaves in winter. They are often found in cold countries, and on high ground.

Firs do not have flowers. They make male and female cones instead. The male cones are small and produce lots of pollen. The female cones are larger and woodier. They catch the pollen from the male cones, and this fertilises an ovule in the cone. A year later the fertilised ovule becomes a small seed with a wing. This is blown away by the wind, and will grow into a new fir tree if it lands on the right soil.

Flies

Flies have a body in three parts: a head, a thorax with wings and six legs, and an abdomen. A house-fly will eat most human food, but it has to make it into a liquid first. To do this it spits on it, then sucks the liquid up. Other flies live on liquids like blood.

When flies mate, sperms from the male fertilise the eggs of a female inside her body. She lays several sets of eggs, with about 100 eggs in each set. They are laid in places like dung heaps. Each egg hatches in a few hours into a tiny worm-like larva. The larva feeds on the dung and grows rapidly. After about five days it makes a hard case round itself, called a pupa. The pupa hatches in three days into an adult fly, which can reproduce in a fortnight.

Flowers

Many plants reproduce by making flowers. The plant usually has green leaves to absorb the sun's energy to make food. These plants also get water and minerals from the soil through roots, and absorb carbon dioxide from the air.

To reproduce, the plant develops male and female parts. The male anthers make pollen. This is carried, usually by insects, to the female parts of another flower. If the pollen reaches the stigma, it grows a tube down to the ovules in the ovary. The male cell from the pollen grain passed down the tube and fertilises an ovule.

When the ovules have been fertilised, the petals die. The ovules grow and become seeds. The seed contains an embryo plant and food for the embryo to start growing. It has a tough coat to protect itself. The ovary with the seeds in also grows. In some plants, like tomatoes, the ovary becomes a fruit which an animal will eat, spreading the seeds. In other plants, like peas and poppies, it becomes a pod that explodes to spread the seeds. Seeds vary in size, from tiny ones like cress seeds, up to coconuts.

Frogs

Frogs are amphibians. The adults live mostly on land, but they reproduce in water. In the spring, male and female frogs move into the water. The male gets on the female's back, and clings on to her with special pads. He does this so that he can put his sperms on the eggs as the female lays them.

The eggs are fertilised in the water. They hatch into tadpoles in about ten days. Young tadpoles eat water plants at first, but after a month or two will eat almost anything. At first they have gills so they can get oxygen from the water, but quite soon they breathe air instead. After growing for two to three months, the tadpole loses its tail. It grows front legs and becomes a young frog. It takes another three years before it can reproduce.

Lice

←————— 1.5mm —————→

Human head lice belong to the louse family of insects. They live in your hair, and their food is your blood, which they suck. Lice have long claws to grip the hair so that they cannot be scratched off, and a tube-like mouth for piercing the skin.

Lice reproduce like other insects. They mate on a person's head. The head-louse lays its eggs in hair, and sticks the eggs to it. The eggs, called nits, hatch in about a week. The warmth of the human body incubates them and they hatch into larvae.

As the larvae grow, they have to change their skins. The old skins are dropped in the hair. In a few weeks the larvae become adults and can reproduce themselves. They cannot move easily, and only spread from one person to another when their hair or bodies touch.

Humans

Humans are one of the world's most successful species. We can reproduce when we choose, and we have no predators (a predator is an animal that feeds on another animal). Human reproduction is described on pages 104–107. The photographs and chart here show how a human develops from a fertilised egg to a mature adult.

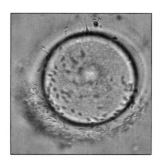

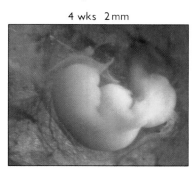
4 wks 2mm

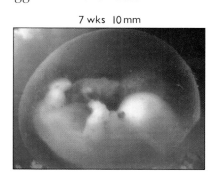
7 wks 10mm

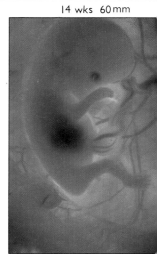
14 wks 60mm

Mushrooms

Mushrooms are a type of fungi. Like all fungi they live on rotting animal and plant matter. The part of the mushroom that you eat is only there to make more mushrooms. Most of the mushroom is a network of tiny tubes under the ground. The tubes absorb organic substances, minerals and water from the soil. This provides food for the mushroom to grow and reproduce.

Fungi reproduce above the ground. As the fungus grows, a cap forms, with gills under it. Spores develop in the gills. The spores are sticky and very small. They drop from the gills and are carried in the wind. When conditions are right, the spores develop the fine tubes that will absorb food and let them grow.

Mushrooms sometimes reproduce sexually. Male and female parts can develop underground.

Some fungi are very poisonous. If you eat a Death Cap or a Fly Agaric toadstool you are likely to die within a day. Other fungi are edible. A fungus called yeast* is important in baking and brewing, and antibiotics are made from a fungus called penicillium.

Slugs

Slugs are very common in the garden. They are mostly plant-eaters, but sometimes they attack small animals like young worms. Like earthworms, slugs are hermaphrodite: a slug has both male and female parts. But they cannot fertilise their own eggs, so they have to mate with another slug to reproduce. Before mating, some types of slug fire a dart into another slug's body. This is probably to make sure that the slugs are of the same type and can mate successfully.

When they mate, the penis of each slug transfers sperms to the female part of the other slug's body. A few hundred eggs are laid in the soil. They are shiny, round and quite small. The larvae develop inside the eggs, which protect them. When the eggs hatch, the slugs are very small, but they have big appetites and quickly grow.

Snakes

Snakes are one of the few groups of animals left from the reptile age 100 million years ago. They have long, flexible backbones, and are nearly all carnivores (meat-eaters). They catch their food either with a poisonous bite or by squeezing the animal and stopping it breathing. They cannot chew food, but swallow it whole. Because a snake has very loose jaws, it can swallow animals that are wider than its own body. Although you may think snakes are nasty and dangerous, most are very shy. The poisonous ones will only bite humans if frightened.

Before mating, male snakes often fight. The winning male lies side by side with the female for several hours. Sperms pass from one of the two penises in the male's tail into the female. The eggs develop inside the female and are then laid in small groups, usually in the ground or under stones. Some snakes incubate their eggs with their bodies, and a few even protect the young for a time after they have hatched.

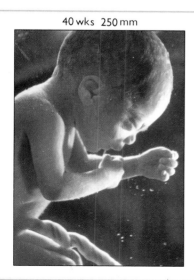

40 wks 250 mm

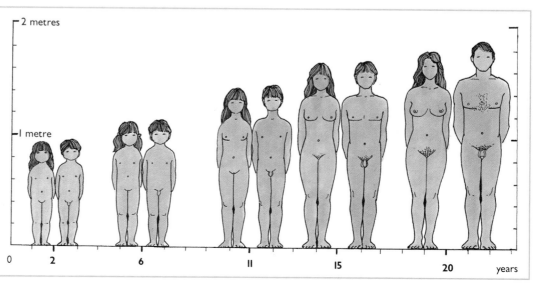

Spiders

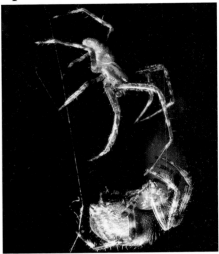

A meadow the size of a hockey pitch will have about 3 million spiders in it. They are very successful animals. A spider has eight jointed legs, a hard outside skeleton and no backbone. Spiders usually have a large body with a small head. Most spiders are carnivorous: they eat other animals. Many spiders make sticky webs to trap their food, then they paralyse it with a poisonous bite.

Male spiders often do a courtship dance before mating. This is not so much to attract the female as to stop her eating him! Before mating, the male prepares a drop of sperm in a small web. When he mates, he places the drop into the female's sex opening. Some female spiders, like the Black Widow, eat the male after mating.

The eggs are fertilised inside the female, and are laid in a silk cocoon. Some species of spider look after their young when they hatch. Others lay more eggs, and then leave them.

Starfish

Starfish live in water. The starfish you sometimes find on the seashore have been stranded by the tide; they cannot live long out of water. Starfish have no backbone, few senses, and no obvious brain. This can cause problems: if a starfish is turned upside down, it has no brain to organise its arms, and they all try to get it the right way up on their own. The starfish can take over an hour to sort itself out. Because of this lack of control, they do not move around much, but wait for food to come near. Starfish live on shellfish like oysters. They pull the shell apart, then eat the animal inside.

There are male and female starfish. The female releases up to two million eggs, and this stimulates the nearby males to produce sperms. Fertilisation happens if a sperm meets an egg in the water. Although many eggs are fertilised, few survive to become adults. Some starfish can reproduce by losing an arm and part of the body. This grows into a new starfish. Most starfish can survive the loss of an arm.

Strawberries

Strawberry plants grow like other flowers*. They have flowers with male and female parts and can reproduce sexually. However, new plants also grow on runners, without any male or female parts being involved. The runners are shoots that grow away from the parent plant. The end of the runner becomes a new strawberry plant, exactly like its parent. Eventually, the runner linking the two plants dies. Runners help strawberries to spread, and make it harder for other plants to grow around them. Buttercups also grow like this.

Sycamore

A sycamore is a deciduous tree. It can grow up to 35m tall and live for several hundred years. Sycamores flower in the summer. The flowers make pollen that is spread from the anthers of one tree to the ovules of another by

insects. The ovaries on the sycamore develop into special fruits to spread the seeds. They form in pairs, with wings. The pairs separate when the fruit is ripe, and they fall from the tree. The wings spin them round, and keep them in the air rather like a helicopter. This gives the wind more chance to spread them away from the parent tree.

Tapeworms

The tapeworm is a parasite: it lives in other animals. A pork tapeworm spends part of its life in a pig, and part in a human.

Pigs eat tapeworm eggs in muddy fields where human sewage has been spread. The eggs develop into larvae that live in the pig's muscle. If the pig is killed and eaten, the cyst starts developing. It hooks itself into the human's intestine and feeds on digested food.

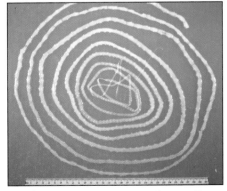

The cyst grows into a long, flat, worm-like body made of segments. The body can grow up to 12 metres long! Each segment has male and female parts, so the sperms from one part can fertilise the eggs from another. When a segment is ripe, thousands of eggs pass down the human's digestive system and out in the human's waste (faeces). If an egg is eaten by a pig, the cycle starts again.

The cyst in the pig is killed if pork is cooked well, so it is important not to eat undercooked pork.

Viruses

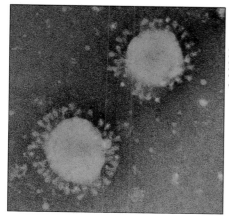

0.00002mm

A virus is the smallest living thing (although some people would say that it is just a bundle of chemicals, and not really alive at all). It is incredibly small: 10 000 viruses end-to-end would just cover a full stop.

Viruses live inside the cells of another organism. The virus is a set of cell plans packed in a protein bag. When the virus is inside a cell, it makes the cell reproduce its plans instead of doing its normal job. This lets the virus multiply to spread to other cells.

Viruses cause many diseases. Colds, flu, measles and rabies are all virus illnesses. The virus spreads from one person to another in droplets in the air, or viruses can be carried by animals. Insects often transfer plant viruses from one plant to another.

Wasps

Most wasps are social insects: they live in nests with up to 5000 other wasps. The nest has a queen wasp whose job is to lay eggs.

Most of the eggs hatch out to become larvae and then sterile female wasps. But in the autumn some fertile males and females also hatch. The males mate with the females, and then die. The females hibernate for the winter; they will start new nests next spring.

Wheat

Like barley, oats and rice, wheat is a grass plant. Together, these crops make up the main part of our diet. All grasses reproduce by making lots of very fine pollen, which is blown into the air by the wind. The pollen causes asthma and hay fever in some people.

To catch the pollen, each plant has a large feathery stigma. If a pollen grain hits this, it sticks and grows a tube down into the ovary. The male cell can then fertilise an ovule and become a seed (called a grain). It is the grain that is used for food. In the wild, the grain could grow into another plant.

Some grasses, like twitch, also spread by growing stems underground. New plants can grow off these. Many garden weeds do this, and spread rapidly.

Woodlice

Woodlice are found in damp places in most gardens. They have a hard shell and jointed legs, but no backbone. Woodlice feed mainly on organic matter like old plants.

There are male and female woodlice. The males have a penis for transferring sperms to the female. After mating, the female carries the fertilised eggs around with her, and the young hatch out in a pouch under the mother. The young woodlice soon leave the mother, but the family often remains in a group for some time.

Yeast

Yeast is a single-cell fungus. It needs sugar and water to grow and reproduce. In a dried form it can survive for many years, but in the right conditions it reproduces very fast by budding. This is a type of simple cell division in which a cell forms within the parent cell, then splits off.

magnified 230 times

Yeast is used to make bread, beer and wine. When it buds it gives off a gas called carbon dioxide. This gas makes bread rise, and it provides the 'fizz' in beer.

Glossary

Abdomen   The bottom part of an animal's body. An insect's abdomen is its tail part. Your abdomen is your belly.

Anther   The part of a plant where pollen is made.

Chromosome   A small thread of chemicals that contains thousands of genes. Organisms that are produced from a male cell and a female cell get one set of chromosomes from the male cell, and one from the female cell. The genes in each chromosome decide what every part of the organism will be like.

Cocoon   A hard outer case in which an insect changes from a larva to an adult.

Cyst   A case that protects an animal.

Fusion   When a male cell and a female cell join together to become a single new cell.

Gene   A tiny part of a chromosome that determines what a particular part of the whole organism will be like.

Hermaphrodite   An animal that has both male and female parts. Usually it cannot fertilise itself, but has to exchange sperms with another animal.

Larva   A stage in an insect's development after hatching. A larva is usually a small crawling or worm-like animal. It will eventually change into an adult that is quite different from the larva.

Organic   Anything that is made from animals and plants.

Ovary   In a plant, the place where the ovules are. In an animal, the place where eggs are made.

Ovule   The female sex cells of a plant.

Penis   A male sex organ used to pass sperms into the female's body.

Pollen   The male sex cells of a plant.

Seed   A fertilised plant cell which has a food store and a coat to protect it.

Sexual reproduction   Animals and plants that pass sex cells from the male part of one organism to the female part of another organism use sexual reproduction.

Sperm   The male sex cell of an animal.

Spore   A cell that a new plant can develop from. It does not have a food store like a seed.

Stigma   The tip of a tube in a plant that leads down to the ovary. It is usually sticky to catch pollen.

Testis   The part of a male animal where sperms are made.

Thorax   The centre part of an animal's body. Your thorax is your chest.

Uterus   The part of a female animal's body where fertilised eggs develop.

Vagina   The part of a female's body that a male animal puts his penis in during mating.

Index

Collins Educational, 8 Grafton Street, London W1X 3LA

© Coles, Gott, Thornley 1988

First published 1988
Reprinted 1989, 1990 (twice)

ISBN 0 00 327431 4

Designed by Wendi Watson

Artwork by Jane Cope, Mike Gordon and PanTek Arts Ltd

Printed and bound in Hong Kong

Typeset by Rowland Phototypesetting Ltd, Bury St Edmunds, Suffolk

Acknowledgements

The authors and publishers are grateful to the following for permission to reproduce photographs on the pages indicated.

(T = top, B = bottom, M = middle, L = left, R = right)

Ardea/Jonathan Player 12T, I. R. Beames 12B, 96TR, 137BR, John Mason 13, 33BL, 141TR, P. Morris 33TL, 56B, 97BL & R, 129, 140TR, 141TM, Anthony and Elizabeth Romford 78BR, J. G. 97TL, Bob Gibbons 136R, 139TM, Jean-Paul Ferrero 137TL, 139TR, Wardene Weisser 137BM, E. Burgess 137TR, Jean-Michel Labat 138TL, Ake Lindau 139TL, J. D. 140BL, D. W. Greenslade 140M
Aviation Photographs International 72BM & R
Barnaby's Picture Library 11BR, 19R, 20, 22M, 30, 37, 38L, 46M & RM, 54 (except hovercraft and bicycle), 56T, 57T, 67L, 68T, 70T, 72BL, 75, 76M & R, 78TM, BL & M, 81TL, 82T, 83, 84, 90B, 91L & R, 96, 108TL, 124, 130
BBC Hulton Picture Library 72T
Dr Alan Beaumont 33BR, 141BL
British Petroleum 76TR
Camera Press 94L
Casio Electronics Co. Ltd 19L
Castrol Ltd 78TL
Central Electricity Generating Board 46B, 47, 57B
Civil Aviation Authority 126
John Cleare 93
Bruce Coleman Ltd/Bill Wood 137BL, Andy Purcell 138TM
Colorsport 10, 65T
Esso Petroleum Co. Ltd 89
Mary Evans Picture Library 76TL, 94R
Fibrax Ltd 23
Ford Motor Company Ltd 11M & BL
Colin Garratt 42

Geological Museum 82B
Gower Medical Publishing Ltd 138BL
Sally and Richard Greenhill 22L & R, 38R, 45, 46TL, TR & BR, 51, 54 (bicycle), 76B, 77L, 78TR, 107B, 108TR & B
Jeremy Hartley/Oxfam 31
Hoverspeed Ltd 54 (hovercraft)
International Museum of Horology, Switzerland 16
LRC Products Ltd 81TM & R
Julia Martin/Photo Co-op 104
Paul Popper Ltd 28
Ann Ronan Picture Library 60, 70B, 133
Royal Society for the Prevention of Accidents 7
Science Photo Library Ltd 65 / John Walsh 33TR, London School of Hygiene and Tropical Medicine 34L, Dr Jeremy Burgess 62, 91LM, 98BL & R, 136TM, 141BR, John Durham 67R, Richard Folwell 68B, Dr R. Clark and M. R. Goff 92, Michael Abbey 98TL, Manfred Kage 98TR, 99, Brian Eyden 98M, S. Grand-Walter 107T, Alex Bartel 116, Martin Bond 121, Jerry Mason 128, Biophoto Associates 136TL, R. B. Taylor 136BL, Tektoff-Merieux, CNRI 136BM, David Spears 137TM, Eric Gravé 138TR, 140BR, Petit Format/Nestlé 138BM & R, 139BL, Martin Dohrn 140TL, 141BM, Dr. S. Patterson 141TL
Ronald Sheridan Photo Library 21, 90T
University of Durham School of Education 122

The authors and publishers would like to thank David and Judith Horner for providing the story on page 106.

Cover
Clockwise from top right: Barnaby's Picture Library, Ford Motor Company Ltd, University of Durham School of Education, Barnaby's Picture Library, Science Photo Library/Jerry Mason, Ann Ronan Picture Library